MW01027924

SHAMBHALA POCKET LIBRARY

THE POCKET

THOMAS MERTON

EDITED WITH AN INTRODUCTION BY

Robert Inchausti

FOREWORD BY

Robert A. F. Thurman

SHAMBHALA · Boulder · 2017

SHAMBHALA PUBLICATIONS, INC.
4720 Walnut Street
Boulder, Colorado 80301
www.shambhala.com

9 8 7 6 5 4 3 2

Printed in the United States of America

⊗ This edition is printed on acid-free paper that meets the
American National Standards Institute z39.48 Standard.
♻ This book is printed on 30% postconsumer recycled paper.
For more information please visit us at www.shambhala.com.
Distributed in the United States by Penguin Random House LLC
and in Canada by Random House of Canada Ltd

Designed by Lora Zorian

THE LIBRARY OF CONGRESS CATALOGUES
THE PREVIOUS EDITON OF THIS BOOK AS FOLLOWS:
Merton, Thomas, 1915–1968.
The pocket Thomas Merton/ edited with an introduction
by Robert Inchausti—1st New Seeds ed.
p. cm.
Abridgement of: Seeds. 1st ed. Boston:
Shambhala Publications, 2002.
Includes bibliographical references.
ISBN 978-1-59030-273-6 (first edition)
ISBN 978-1-61180-376-1 (Shambhala Pocket Library)
1. Spiritual life—Catholic Church. I. Inchausti, Robert, 1952– II.
Merton, Thomas, 1915–1968. Seeds. III. Title.
bx2350.3.m47 2005
242—dc22

The purpose of a book of meditations is to teach you how to think and not to do your thinking for you. Consequently if you pick up such a book and simply read it through, you are wasting your time. As soon as any thought stimulates your mind or your heart you can put the book down because your meditation has begun. To think that you are somehow obliged to follow the author of the book to his own particular conclusion would be a great mistake. It may happen that his conclusion does not apply to you. God may want you to end up somewhere else. He may have planned to give you quite a different grace than the one the author suggests you might be needing. (NS 215)

CONTENTS

FOREWORD

This book's epigraph (page v) says it all, in a way. Merton wants us to find God and His grace in our own ways, and he is visualizing the reader as a living spiritual being who is meeting him through the words he writes. This explains why he is such a great writer—he is talking personally to me and you! *He* is disclaiming his own wisdom about what you and I need, though he is stepping in to inspire us to find it on our own, spurred by something he reflects to us. "God's grace" is what he thinks can do us good, by which he affirms his faith in an underlying power and force for goodness in the universe that is there for us, beneath the vale of suffering we often feel trapped in. He implies that any of us, should we despair of our holding on to anything else—anything at all, even life or even death—have a fallback situation where we will be buoyed up on the flowing grace of this force for goodness, which he calls "God," as do a great many.

This faith of his in the fundamental goodness of the universe, in a way beyond the universe (perhaps I should say the "Deiverse" or "Theoverse," as they seem to be to the truly faithful), may be the reason that Merton came to love the Buddha. In the journey he made, during which he accidentally and tragically passed away from us too soon, he experienced an epiphany of God's grace in front of the great stone sculpture of the reclining, full-nirvana-attaining, parinirvāna Buddha at Polonnaruwa in Sri Lanka. He then journeyed to North India, to Dharamsala, where he met—and also loved and was loved by—His Holiness the Dalai Lama, then a youngster of barely thirty years. Merton the Christian monk was able to inspire Tenzin Gyatso, the Shakya mendicant, to the effect that there are many paths to holiness, to salvation, to enlightenment. His Holiness often says that he found a genuine enlightenment in Merton, meaning a deep wisdom, a true love and compassion, and a gracious and humorous humility. This meant to His Holiness, as he freely admits, that his inherited idea that only Buddha's teaching can lead to true enlightenment was incorrect, and that the world really does need a true plurality and friendly kinship of faiths. On Merton's side, it seems he found a great soul, young and still learning about the harsh world that was causing him and his people a great deal of suffering, but who was reacting to it with compassion and determination that good could be found amid the pain. Merton went on to meet senior Tibetan lamas, some with great contemplative experience, especially the most venerable Chatral Rinpoche, who deeply moved Merton with his presence, a field of grace from decades of meditative retreat that resonated with the Cistercian contemplative.

When Merton was accidentally electrocuted soon after that meeting in Thailand, it closed off the writings he was about to deliver in which he undoubtedly would have made great contributions to the world's vision of a true kinship of mutually respected faiths. We must regret that we were able to have no further writings from him after that. But what we do have here, in this book, a quintessential cream of his reflective kindness, is certainly rewarding enough and teaches us powerfully where we most importantly must look for truth, reality, and grace: within. Each of us must look within to find our deepest nature, freedom, joy, and the natural true concern for others that is the key to life. That search is expressed so well in this passage:

> True solitude is selfless. Therefore, it is rich in silence and charity and peace. It finds in itself seemingly inexhaustible resources of good to bestow on other people. False solitude is self-centered. And because it finds nothing in its own center, it seeks to draw all things into itself. But everything it touches becomes infected with its own nothingness, and falls apart.

The Buddha's and the Christ's great insights and teachings of what is called "the true self of selflessness" could not be more simply, powerfully, and exquisitely put into words. This teaching is a precious gem. I welcome it and the many other heart-healing, medicine teachings in this book, and am honored to write this little foreword to pay my respects to this great being Thomas Merton and to his honest, gifted, and skilled disciple who selected the precious paragraphs herein, and to invite us all to read and contemplate with this jewel-book again and again.

Robert A. F. Thurman

Jey Tsong Khapa Professor of Buddhist Studies,
Columbia University
President, Tibet House US
September 17, 2016

INTRODUCTION

On September 25, 2015—the centennial year of Thomas Merton's birth—Pope Francis addressed a joint session of the United States Congress. In that speech, he named Thomas Merton as one of the four great, prophetic figures in American history—along with Abraham Lincoln, Martin Luther King Jr., and Dorothy Day.

The pope even quoted from the opening paragraph of Merton's autobiography *The Seven Storey Mountain*:

> I came into the world free by nature, in the image of God. I was, nevertheless, the prisoner of my own violence and my own selfishness, in the image of the world into which I was born; that world was the picture of Hell, full of men like myself, loving God, and yet hating him; born to love him, living instead in fear and hopeless self-contradictory hungers.

It was an apt citation highlighting one of the great themes of the pope's pontificate: namely, that by our own ambition and untethered pride, we have alienated ourselves from God's mercy.

A few months after the pope's speech to Congress,

an avant-garde theatrical piece celebrating Merton's one-hundredth birthday—*The Glory of the World*—opened off-Broadway. It featured an all-male cast of young hipsters who ate cake and ice cream, wore beards, played with balloons, and bounced around on a blow-up mattress. Toasts were given in Merton's honor, and arguments erupted over the meaning of his life legacy. One advertisement for the play summarized its thesis: "What makes a man? What makes a saint? What if nothing is sacred—and everything is?"

The playwright, Charles L. Mee, was not interested in painting a portrait of "the essential Merton," but rather in dramatizing the questions, conversations, and controversies inspired by him. Indeed, the play suggests that no such "essential Merton" can be found and, perhaps, none needed.

Suddenly the curious figure of Thomas Merton—world-famous hermit, bohemian poet, and anti-war activist—was in the news again, and at a time that coincided with hundreds of serious academic conferences, retreats, and publications reconsidering his effect on the last one hundred years.

One of the most notable conferences was the fourteenth general meeting of the International Thomas Merton Society held in Louisville, Kentucky. This impressive meeting of Merton scholars included former Archbishop of Canterbury Ret. Rev. Rowan Williams whose plenary address "Words, War, and Silence: Thomas Merton for the Twenty-First Century" was tweeted live over the World Wide Web.

Rev. Williams—one of Merton's most perceptive readers—once famously remarked that:

> being interested in Merton is *not* being interested in an original, (or) "shaping mind," but being interested in God and human possibilities. Merton will not let (us) look at him for long: he will, finally, persuade (us) to look in the direction he is looking.[*]

It is a point often acknowledged by Merton scholars that Merton's signature accomplishment was not the expression of any peculiarity of outlook or iconoclasm in point view, but rather the lucidity of his intellect and the unflinching purity of his mysticism. Merton was a thinker of such unfettered spiritual focus that virtually everything he ever wrote about—from poem to memoir to essay—held true to the ever-elusive transcendental Absolute. He was exemplary as a theorist, not because his sanctity made him superior to others, but because it made it possible for him to discern the jeweled center of the mind lurking in and around the claims and assertions of everybody else. This is why

[*] *A Silent Action* (London: SPCK, 2013), 19.

Father Nouwen described Merton as inaugurating a new vocation—that of "contemplative critic," monk as public intellectual.

Rowan Williams's centennial speech focused on Merton's analysis of the "death-dealing banality" of modern political speech. We need, Merton had argued, new forms of listening and communicating that shifted our attention from the categories and concerns of the powerful to those of the powerless. In an age of "dark money," Citizens United, and mass-mediate demagoguery, there was, Williams suggested, no more pressing social need.

Merton's own solution to this problem is, perhaps, best illustrated by his interfaith dialogues with Jewish mystics and Buddhist and Sufi contemplatives. In a special edition of *Buddhist-Christian Studies* dedicated to interfaith dialogue, Judith Simmer-Brown examined Merton's friendship with Tibetan Buddhist Chögyam Trungpa as the prototype for a kind of communication based less on an exchange of ideas or any search for rational dialectical synthesis than on an attempt at mutual understanding and respect for differences. Merton's conversations with Trungpa did not broker any metaphysical agreements, but rather they documented common concerns and shared astonishments.

What follows here are some of the spiritual insights and astonishments of Thomas Merton arranged in the most logical pattern I could fashion. Admittedly, such a strategy belies Merton's own digressive approach, but any false impression as to his personal style of writing can be easily corrected by reading one of Merton's discursive essays in its entirety. No attempt is made to summarize his thoughts or condense his life's achievements; rather, this is merely a representative sample of some of his best ideas and most eloquent prose—a collection of jewels rather than a ledger of holdings.

Of all the genres Merton sampled, the "paragraph" was his forte—brilliant, dialogical paragraphs in which the whole of an essay found itself contained and expressed holistically. Composed more in the spirit of a Shakespearean sonnet than a Hegelian "sentence," Merton's paragraphs document spiritual paradoxes, ironies, and unexpected designs and graces rather than chase down logical twists and turns. They are the reflections of a poet more than a philosopher and the speculations of an essayist linking thought to experience rather than the theses of a theologian seeking authority through argument.

If there is any overarching organizing principle to the passages collected here, any single unifying idea, it may simply be that discovering the contemplative life was, for Thomas Merton, "a new self-discovery . . . the flowering of a deeper identity on an entirely different plane." (CIWA 349) And this paradoxical new self—found in the loss of self—led him to a pure and startling new depth of understanding.

Becoming a writer had initiated Merton to a life of self-reflection. And becoming a contemplative Catholic monk ordered that life to the mysteries and designs of Divine Providence. If you have never read Thomas Merton before, hold onto your hat, because the spiritual life, as he describes it, is no litany of pieties but rather a call to fearless intellectual honesty and unfettered self-expression. Merton tells us things not usually found in spiritual books—unsettling things about ourselves, the world, and the impenetrable mysteries of grace.

In his preface to the Japanese edition of *The Seven Storey Mountain*, Merton described his ambitions as a writer this way:

It is not as an author that I would speak to you, not as a story-teller, not as a philosopher, not as a friend only: I seek to speak to you, in some way, as your own self. Who can tell what this may mean? I myself do not know. But if you listen, things will be said that are perhaps not written in this book. And this will be due not to me, but to One who lives and speaks in both. (HR 67)

Amen.

Robert Inchausti
San Luis Obispo, California

PART ONE

REAL AND FALSE SELVES

At the heart of Merton's spirituality is his distinction between our real and false selves. Our false selves are the identities we cultivate in order to function in society with pride and self-possession; our real selves are a deep religious mystery, known entirely only to God. The world cultivates the false self, ignores the real one, and therein lies the great irony of human existence: the more we make of ourselves, the less we actually exist.

All sin starts from the assumption that my false self, the self that exists only in my own egocentric desires, is the fundamental reality of life to which everything else in the universe is ordered. Thus I use up my life in the desire for pleasures and the thirst for experiences, for power, honor, knowledge, and love to clothe this false self and construct its nothingness into something objectively real. And I wind experiences around myself and cover myself with pleasures and glory like bandages in order to make myself perceptible to myself and to the world, as if I were an invisible body that could only become visible when something visible covered its surface. (NS 34–35)

————

If we take our vulnerable shell to be our true identity, if we think our mask is our true face, we will protect it with fabrications even at the cost of violating our own truth. This seems to be the collective endeavor of society: the more busily men dedicate themselves to it, the more certainly it becomes a collective illusion, until in the end we have the enormous, obsessive, uncontrollable dynamic of fabrications designed to protect mere fictitious identities—"selves," that is to say, regarded as objects. Selves that can stand back and see themselves having fun (an illusion which reassures them that they are real). (RU 15)

————

To say I was born in sin is to say I came into the world with a false self. I was born in a mask. I came into existence under a sign of contradiction, being someone that I was never intended to be and therefore a denial of what I am supposed to be. And thus I came into existence and nonexistence at the same time because from the very start I was something that I was not. (NS 33–34)

———

The deep secrecy of my own being is often hidden from me by my own estimate of what I am. My idea of what I am is falsified by my admiration for what I do. And my illusions about myself are bred by contagion from the illusions of other men. We all seek to imitate one another's imagined greatness. If I do not know who I am, it is because I think I am the sort of person everyone around me wants to be. Perhaps I have never asked myself whether I really wanted to become what everybody else seems to want to become. Perhaps if I only realized that I do not admire what everyone seems to admire, I would really begin to live after all. I would be liberated from the painful duty of saying what I really do not think and acting in a way that betrays God's truth and the integrity of my own soul. (NM 125–126)

———

Every one of us is shadowed by an illusory person: a false self. This is the man that I want to be but who cannot exist, because God does not know anything about him. And to be unknown of God is altogether too much privacy. (NS 34)

———————

The earthly desires men cherish are shadows. There is no true happiness in fulfilling them. Why, then, do we continue to pursue joys without substance? Because the pursuit itself has become our only substitute for joy. Unable to rest in anything we achieve, we determine to forget our discontent in a ceaseless quest for new satisfactions. In this pursuit, desire itself becomes our chief satisfaction." (ATT 17)

———————

There is a paradox that lies in the very heart of human existence. It must be apprehended before any lasting happiness is possible in the soul of a man. The paradox is this: man's nature, by itself, can do little or nothing to settle his most important problems. If we follow nothing but our natures, our own philosophies, our own level of ethics, we will end up in hell.

This would be a depressing thought, if it were not purely abstract. Because in the concrete order of things God gave man a nature that was ordered to a supernatural life. He created man with a soul that was

made not to bring itself to perfection in its own order, but to be perfected by Him in an order infinitely
beyond the reach of human powers. We were never
destined to lead purely natural lives, and therefore we
were never destined in God's plan for a purely natural
beatitude. Our nature, which is a free gift of God, was
given us to be perfected and enhanced by another free
gift that is not due it." (SSM 169)

———

To start with one's ego-identity and to try to bring that
identity to terms with external reality by thinking, and
then, having worked out practical principles, to act on
reality from one privileged autonomous position—in
order to bring it into line with an absolute good we
have arrived at by thought: this is the way we become
irresponsible. If reality is something we interpret and
act on to suit our own concept of ourselves, we "respond" to nothing. We simply dictate our own terms,
and "realism" consists in keeping the terms somewhat
plausible. But this implies no real respect for reality,
for other persons, for their needs, and in the end it
implies no real respect for ourselves, since, without
bothering to question the deep mystery of our own
identity, we fabricate a trifling and impertinent identity for ourselves with the bare scraps of experience
that we find lying within immediate reach. (CGB 242)

———————

If we want to understand alienation, we have to find where its deepest taproot goes—and we have to realize that this root will always be there. Alienation is inseparable from culture, from civilization, and from life in society. It is not just a feature of "bad" cultures, "corrupt" civilizations, or urban society. It is not just a dubious privilege reserved for some people in society . . . Alienation begins when culture divides me against myself, puts a mask on me, gives me a role I may or may not want to play. Alienation is complete when I become completely identified with my mask, totally satisfied with my role, and convince myself that any other identity or role is inconceivable. The man who sweats under his mask, whose role makes him itch with discomfort, who hates the division in himself, is already beginning to be free. But God help him if all he wants is the mask the other man is wearing, just because the other one does not seem to be sweating or itching. Maybe he is no longer human enough to itch. (Or else he pays a psychiatrist to scratch him.)   (LE 381)

———————

The way to find the real "world" is not merely to measure and observe what is outside us, but to discover our own inner ground. For that is where the world is, *first* of all: in my deepest self. This "ground," this "world" where I am mysteriously present at once to my own self and to the freedoms of all other men, is not a visible, objective and determined structure with fixed laws and demands. It is a living and self-creating mystery of which I am myself a part, to which I am myself my own unique door. (CIWA 154–155)

––––––––

The shallow "I" of individualism can be possessed, developed, cultivated, and pandered to, satisfied: it is the center of all our strivings for gains and for satisfaction, whether material or spiritual. But the deep "I" of the spirit, of solitude and of love, cannot be "had," possessed, developed, perfected. It can only be and act according to the inner laws which are not of man's contriving but which come from God. They are the Laws of the Spirit who, like the wind, blows where He wills. This inner "I," who is always alone, is always universal: for in this most inmost "I" my own solitude meets the solitude of every other man and the solitude of God. Hence it is beyond division, beyond limitation, beyond selfish affirmation. (DQ 207)

––––––––

There is and can be no special planned technique for discovering and awakening one's inner self, because the inner self is first of all a spontaneity that is nothing if not free. Therefore there is no use in trying to start with a definition of the inner self, and then deducing from its essential properties some appropriate and infallible means of submitting it to control—as if the essence could give us some clue to that which is vulnerable in it, something we can lay hold of, in order to gain power over it. Such an idea would imply a complete misapprehension of the existential reality we are talking about. The inner self is not a part of our being, like a motor in a car. It is our entire substantial reality itself, on its highest and most personal and most existential level. It is like life, and it is life: it is our spiritual life when it is most alive. It is the life by which everything else in us lives and moves. It is in and through and beyond everything that we are. If it is awakened it communicates a new life to the intelligence in which it lives, so that it becomes a living awareness of itself: and this awareness is not so much something that we ourselves have, as something that we are. It is a new and indefinable quality of our Living being.

The inner self is as secret as God and, like Him, it evades every concept that tries to seize hold of it with full possession. It is a life that cannot be held and studied as object, because it is not "a thing." It is not reached and coaxed forth from hiding by any process under the sun, including meditation. All that we can do with any spiritual discipline is produce within ourselves something of the silence, the humility, the detachment, the purity of heart and the indifference which are required if the inner self is to make some predictable manifestation of his Presence. (CQR 5–6)

————

We do not have to create a conscience for ourselves. We are born with one, and no matter how much we may ignore it, we cannot silence its insistent demand that we do good and avoid evil. No matter how much we may deny our freedom and our moral responsibility, our intellectual soul cries out for a morality and a spiritual freedom without which it knows it cannot be happy. (NM 41–42)

————

In our being there is a primordial *yes* that is not our own; it is not at our own disposal; it is not accessible to our inspection and understanding; we do not even fully experience it as real (except in rare and unique circumstances). And we have to admit that for most people this primordial "yes" is something they never advert to at all. It is in fact absolutely unconscious, totally forgotten.

Basically, however, my being is not an affirmation of a limited self, but the "yes" of Being itself, irrespective of my own choices. Where do "I" come in? Simply in uniting the "yes" of my own freedom with the "yes" of Being that already *is* before I have a chance to choose.

This is not "adjustment." There is nothing to adjust. There is reality, and there is free consent. There is the actuality of one "yes." In this actuality no question of "adjustment" remains and the ego vanishes. (CGB 243)

———————

Our being is not to be enriched merely by activity and experience as such. Everything depends on the quality of our acts and our experiences. A multitude of badly performed actions and of experiences only half-lived exhausts and depletes our being. By doing things badly we make ourselves less real. This growing unreality cannot help but make us unhappy and fill us with a sense of guilt. But the purity of our conscience has a natural proportion with the depth of our being and the quality of our acts: and when our activity is habitually disordered, our malformed conscience can think of nothing better to tell us than to multiply the quantity of our acts, without perfecting their quality. *And* so we go from bad to worse, exhaust ourselves, empty our whole life of all content, and fall into despair. There are times, then, when in order to keep ourselves in existence at all we simply have to sit back for a while and do nothing. And for a man who has let himself be drawn completely out of himself by his activity, nothing is more difficult than to sit still and rest, doing nothing at all. The very act of resting is the hardest and most courageous act he can perform: and often it is quite beyond his power. We must first recover the possession of our own being (NM 123)

———————

The first step in the interior life, nowadays, is not as some might imagine, learning not to see and taste and hear and feel things. On the contrary, what we must do is begin unlearning our wrong ways of seeing, tasting, feeling, and so forth, and acquire a few of the right ones.

For asceticism is not merely a matter of renouncing television, cigarettes, and gin. Before we can begin to be ascetics, we first have to learn to see life as if it were something more than a hypnotizing telecast. And we must be able to taste something besides tobacco and alcohol: we must perhaps even be able to taste these luxuries themselves as if they too were good.

How can our conscience tell us whether or not we are renouncing things unless it first tells us how to use them properly? For renunciation is not an end in itself: it helps us to use things better. It helps us to give them away. If reality revolts us, if we merely turn away from it in disgust, to whom shall we sacrifice it? How shall we consecrate it? How shall we make of it a gift to God and to men? (NM 33–34)

———————

True solitude is found in humility, which is infinitely rich. False solitude is the refuge of pride, and it is infinitely poor. The poverty of false solitude comes from an illusion which pretends, by adorning itself in things it can never possess, to distinguish one individual self from the mass of other men. True solitude is selfless. Therefore, it is rich in silence and charity and peace. It finds in itself seemingly inexhaustible resources of good to bestow on other people. False solitude is self-centered. And because it finds nothing in its own center, it seeks to draw all things into itself. But everything it touches becomes infected with its own nothingness, and falls apart. True solitude cleans the soul, lays it wide open to the four winds of generosity. False solitude locks the door against all men and pores over its own private accumulation of rubbish.   (NM 248–249)

———

The things we really need come to us only as gifts, and in order to receive them as gifts we have to be open. In order to be open we have to renounce ourselves, in a sense we have to *die* to our image of ourselves, our autonomy, our fixation upon our self-willed identity. We have to be able to relax the psychic and spiritual cramp which knots us in the painful, vulnerable, helpless "I" that is all we know as ourselves.   (CGB 204)

———

The heresy of individualism: thinking oneself a completely self-sufficient unit and asserting this imaginary "unity" against all others. The affirmation of the self as simply "not the other." But when you seek to affirm your unity by denying that you have anything to do with anyone else, by negating everyone else in the universe until you come down to *you:* what is there left to affirm? Even if there were something to affirm, you would have no breath left with which to affirm it. The true way is just the opposite: the more I am able to affirm others, to say "yes" to them in myself, by discovering them in myself and myself in them, the more real I am. I am fully real if my own heart says *yes* to *everyone.* I will be a better Catholic, not if I can *refute* every shade of Protestantism, but if I can affirm the truth in it and still go further. So, too, with the Muslims, the Hindus, the Buddhists, etc. This does not mean syncretism, indifferentism, the vapid and careless friendliness that accepts everything by thinking of nothing. There is much that one cannot "affirm" and "accept," but first one must say "yes" where one really can. If I affirm myself as a Catholic merely by denying all that is Muslim, Jewish, Protestant, Hindu, Buddhist, etc., in the end I will find that there is not much left for me to affirm as a Catholic: and certainly no breath of the Spirit with which to affirm it.   (CGB 128–129)

We ought to have the humility to admit we do not know all about ourselves, that we are not experts at running our own lives. We ought to stop taking our conscious plans and decisions with such infinite seriousness. It may well be that we are *not* the martyrs or the mystics or the apostles or the leaders or the lovers of God that we imagine ourselves to be. Our subconscious mind may be trying to tell us this in many ways and we have trained, ourselves, with the most egregious self-righteousness to turn a deaf ear. (NM 38)

The problem is to learn how to renounce resentment without selling out to the organization people who want everyone to accept absurdity and moral anarchy in a spirit of uplift and willing complicity. (NS 109)

The only true joy on earth is to escape from the prison of our own false self, and enter by love into union with the Life Who dwells and sings within the essence of every creature and in the core of our own souls. In His love we possess all things and enjoy fruition of them, finding Him in them all. And thus as we go about the world, everything we meet and everything we see and hear and touch, far from defiling, purifies us and plants in us something more of contemplation and of heaven.

Short of this perfection, created things do not bring us joy but pain. Until we love God perfectly, everything in the world will be able to hurt us. And the greatest misfortune is to be dead to the pain they inflict on us, and not to realize what it is.

For until we love God perfectly His world is full of contradiction. The things He has created attract us to Him and yet keep us away from Him. They draw us on and they stop us dead. We find Him in them to some extent and then we don't find Him in them at all. Just when we think we have discovered some joy in them, the joy turns into sorrow; and just when they are beginning to please us the pleasure turns into pain. In all created things we, who do not yet perfectly love God, can find something that reflects the fulfillment of heaven and something that reflects the anguish of hell. We find something of the joy of blessedness and something of the pain of loss, which is damnation. The fulfillment we find in creatures belongs to the reality of the created being, a reality that is from God and belongs to God and reflects God. The anguish we find in them belongs to the disorder of our desire which looks for a greater reality in the object of our desire than is actually there: a greater fulfillment than any created thing is capable of giving. Instead of worshipping God through His creation we are always trying to worship ourselves by means of creatures.   (NS 25, 26)

PART TWO

THE WORLD WE LIVE IN

Thomas Merton's view of the modern world evolved over time from a stark rejection of its empty promises to a deep compassion for its tragic limitations. In the passages that follow, Merton tries to provide a larger social and spiritual context to life in the modern world.

UNREAL CITY

We are living in the greatest revolution in history—a huge spontaneous upheaval of the entire human race: not the revolution planned and carried out by any particular party, race, or nation, but a deep elemental boiling over of all the inner contradictions that have ever been in man, a revelation of the chaotic forces inside everybody. This is not something we have chosen, nor is it something we are free to avoid.

This revolution is a profound spiritual crisis of the whole world, manifested largely in desperation, cynicism, violence, conflict, self-contradiction, ambivalence, fear and hope, doubt and belief, creation and destructiveness, progress and regression, obsessive attachments to images, idols, slogans, programs that only dull the general anguish for a moment until it bursts out everywhere in a still more acute and terrifying form. We do not know if we are building a fabulously wonderful world or destroying all that we have ever had, all that we have achieved! All the inner force of man is boiling and bursting out, the good together with the evil, the good poisoned by evil and fighting it, the evil pretending to be good and revealing itself in the most dreadful crimes, justified and rationalized by the purest and most innocent intentions.   (CGB 54–55)

––––––––

The real trouble with "the world," in the bad sense which the Gospel condemns, is that it is a complete and systematic sham, and he who follows it ends not by living but by pretending he is alive, and justifying his pretense by an appeal to the general conspiracy of all the others to do the same.

It is this pretense that must be vomited out in the desert.[1] But when the monastery is only a way station to the desert, when it remains permanently that and nothing else, then one is neither in the world nor out of it. One lives marginally, with one foot in the general sham. (CGB 310)

––––––––

The city itself lives on its own myth. Instead of waking up and silently existing, the city people prefer a stubborn and fabricated dream; they do not care to be a part of the night, or to be merely of the world. They have constructed a world outside the world, against the world, a world of mechanical fictions which condemn nature and only to use it up, thus preventing it from renewing itself and man. (RU 10–11)

––––––––

We live in a society whose whole policy is to excite every nerve in the human body and keep it at the highest pitch of artificial tension, to strain every human desire to the limit and to create as many new desires and synthetic passions as possible, in order to cater to them with the products of our factories and printing presses and movie studios. (SSM 133)

———————

We live in a society that tries to keep us dazzled with euphoria in a bright cloud of lively and joy-loving slogans. Yet nothing is more empty and more dead, nothing is more insultingly insincere and destructive than the vapid grins on the billboards and the moron beatitudes in the magazines which assure us that we are all in bliss right now. I know of course that we are fools, but I do not think any of us are fools enough to believe that we are now in heaven, even though the Russians are breaking their necks in order to become as rich as we are. I think the constant realization that we are exhausting our vital spiritual energy in a waste of shame, the inescapable disgust at the idolatrous vulgarity of our commercial milieu (or the various other apocalyptic whoredoms that abound elsewhere on the face of the earth) is one of the main sources of our universal desperation. (FAV 116)

———————

If we are fools enough to remain at the mercy of the people who want to sell us happiness, it will be impossible for us ever to be content with anything. How would they profit if we became content? We would no longer need their new product.

The last thing the salesman wants is for the buyer to become content. You are of no use in our affluent society unless you are always just about to grasp what you never have.

The Greeks were not as smart as we are. In their primitive way they put Tantalus[2] in hell. Madison Avenue, on the contrary, would convince us that Tantalus is in heaven.   (CGB 84)

––––––

The population of the affluent world is nourished on a steady diet of brutal mythology and hallucination, kept at a constant pitch of high tension by a life that is intrinsically violent in that it forces a large part of the population to submit to an existence which is humanly intolerable. . . . The problem of violence, then, is not the problem of a few rioters and rebels, but the problem of a whole structure which is outwardly ordered and respectable, and inwardly ridden by psychopathic obsessions and delusions.   (FAV 3)

––––––

I have learned that an age in which politicians talk about peace is an age in which everybody expects war: the great men of the earth would not talk of peace so much if they did not secretly believe it possible, with *one more war,* to annihilate their enemies forever. Always, "after just one more war" it will dawn, the new era of love: but first everybody who is hated must be eliminated. For hate, you see, is the mother of their kind of love.

Unfortunately the love that is to be born out of hate will never be born. Hatred is sterile; it breeds nothing but the image of its own empty fury, its own nothingness. Love cannot come of emptiness. It is full of reality. Hatred destroys the real being of man in fighting the fiction which it calls "the enemy." For man is concrete and alive, but "the enemy" is a subjective abstraction. A society that kills real men in order to deliver itself from the phantasm of a paranoid delusion is already possessed by the demon of destructiveness because it has made itself incapable of love. It refuses, *a priori,* to love. It is dedicated not to concrete relations of man with man, but only to abstractions about politics, economics, psychology, and even, sometimes, religion. (CP 374–375)

———

This is no longer a time of systematic ethical specula-tion, for such speculation implies time to reason, and the power to bring social and individual action under the concerted control of reasoned principles upon which most men agree. There is no time to reason out, calmly and objectively, the moral implications of techni-cal developments which are perhaps already superseded by the time one knows enough to reason about them.

Action is not governed by moral reason but by political expediency and the demands of technol-ogy—translated into the simple abstract formulas of propaganda. These formulas have nothing to do with reasoned moral action, even though they may appeal to apparent moral values—they simply condition the mass of men to react in a desired way to certain stim-uli.   (CGB 53–54)

———

In our society, a society of business rooted in Puri-tanism, based on a pseudo-ethic of industriousness and thrift, to be rewarded by comfort, pleasure, and a good bank account, the myth of work is thought to justify an existence that is essentially meaningless and futile. There is, then, a great deal of busy-ness as people invent things to do when in fact there is very little to be done. Yet we are overt, whelmed with jobs, duties, tasks, assignments, "missions" of every kind. At every moment we are sent north, south, east, and west by the angels of business and art, poetry and politics, science and war, to the four corners of the universe to decide something, to sign something, to buy and sell. We fly in all directions to sell ourselves, thus justifying the absolute nothingness of our lives. The more we seem to accomplish, the harder it becomes to really dissimulate our trifling, and the only thing that saves us is the common conspiracy not to advert to what is really going on. (CGB 177)

———

Businesses are, in reality, quasi-religious sects. When you go to work in one you embrace *a new faith*. And if they are really big businesses, you progress from faith to a kind of mystique. Belief in the product, preaching the product, in the end the product becomes the focus of a transcendental experience. Through "the product" one communes with the vast forces of life, nature, and history that are expressed in business. Why not face it? Advertising treats all products with the reverence and the seriousness due to sacraments.

Harrington says *(Life in the Crystal Palace)*: "The new evangelism whether expressed in soft or hard selling, is a quasi-religious approach to business, wrapped in a hoax—a hoax voluntarily entered into by producers and consumers together. Its credo is that of belief-to-order. It is the truth-to-order as delivered by advertising and public relations men, believed in by them and voluntarily believed by the public."[3] Once again, it is the question of a game. Life is aimless, but one invents a thousand aimless aims and then mobilizes a whole economy around them, finally declaring them to be transcendental, mystical, and absolute.

Compare our monastery and the General Electric plant in Louisville. Which one is the more serious and more "religious" institution? One might be tempted to say "the monastery," out of sheer habit. But, in fact, the religious seriousness of the monastery is like sandlot baseball compared with the big-league seriousness of General Electric. It may in face occur to many, including the monks, to *doubt* the monastery and what it represents. Who doubts G.E.? (CGB 211)

––––––––

Popular religion has to a great extent betrayed man's inner spirit and turned him over, like Samson, with his hair cut off and his eyes dug out, to turn the mill of a self-frustrating and self-destroying culture. The clichés of popular religion have in many cases become every bit as hollow and as false as those of soap salesmen, and far more dangerously deceptive because one cannot so easily verify the claims made about the product. The sin of religiosity is that it has turned God, peace, happiness, salvation and all that man desires into products to be marketed in an especially attractive package deal. In this, I think, the fault lies not with the sincerity of preachers and religious writers, but with the worn-out presuppositions with which they fare content to operate. The religious mind today is seldom pertinently or prophetically critical. Oh, it is critical all right; but too often of wrong or irrelevant issues. There is still such a thing as straining at gnats and swallowing camels. But I wonder if we have not settled down too comfortably to accept passively the prevarications that the Gospels or the Prophets would have us reject with all the strength of our being. I am afraid the common combination of organizational jollity, moral legalism and nuclear crusading will not pass muster as a serious religion. It certainly has little to do with "spiritual life." (FAV 116–117)

————

We are all the more inclined to idolatry because we imagine that we are of all generations the most enlightened, the most objective, the most scientific, the most progressive and the most humane. This, in fact, is an "image" of ourselves—an image which is false and is also the object of a cult. We worship ourselves in this image. The nature of our acts is determined in large measure by the demands of our worship. Because we have an image (simulacrum) of ourselves as fair, objective, practical and humane, we actually make it more difficult for ourselves to be what we think we are.

Since our "objectivity" for instance is in fact an image of ourselves as "objective," we soon take our objectivity for granted, and instead of checking the facts, we simply manipulate the facts to fit our pious conviction. In other words, instead of taking care to examine the realities of our political or social problems, we simply bring out the idols in solemn procession. "We are the ones who are right, they are the ones who are wrong. We are the good guys, they are the bad guys. We honest, they are crooks." In this confrontation of images, "objectivity" ceases to be a consistent attention to fact and becomes a devout and blind fidelity to myth. If the adversary is by definition wicked, then objectivity consists simply in refusing to believe that he can possibly be honest in any circumstances whatever. If facts seem to conflict with images, then we feel that we are being tempted by the devil, and we determine that we will be all the more blindly loyal to our images. To debate with the devil would be to yield! Thus in support of realism and objectivity we simply determine beforehand that we will be swayed by no fact whatever that does not accord perfectly with our own preconceived judgment. Objectivity becomes simple dogmatism.   (FAV 154–155)

———

Is there any vestige of truth left in our declaration that we think for ourselves? Or do we even trouble to declare this any more? Perhaps the man who says he "thinks for himself" is simply one who does not think at all because he has no fully articulate thoughts, he thinks he has his own incommunicable ideas. Or thinks that, if he once set his mind to it, he could have his own thoughts. But he just has not got around to doing this. I wonder if "democracies" are made up entirely of people who "think for themselves" in the sense of going around with blank minds which they imagine they could fill with their own thoughts if need be.

Well, the need has been desperately urgent, not for one year or ten, but for fifty, sixty, seventy, a hundred years. If, when thought is needed, nobody does any *thinking*, if everyone assumes that someone else is thinking, then it is clear that no one is thinking either for himself or for anybody else. Instead of thought; there is a vast, inhuman void full of words, formulas, slogans, declarations, echoes—ideologies! You can always reach out and help yourself to some of them. You don't even have to reach at all. Appropriate echoes already rise up in your mind—they are "yours." You realize of course that these are not yet "thoughts." Yet we "think" these formulas, with which the void in our hearts is provisionally entertained, can for the time being "take the place of thoughts"—while the computers make decisions for us. (CGB 66)

———

A few years ago a man who was compiling a book entitled *Success* wrote and asked me to contribute a statement on how I got be a success. I replied indignantly that I was not able to consider myself a success in any terms that had a meaning to me. I swore I had spent my life strenuously avoiding success. If it so happened that I had once written a best seller, this was a pure accident, due to inattention and naiveté, and I would take very good care never to do the same again. If I had a message to my contemporaries, I said, it was surely this: Be anything you like, be madmen, drunks, and bastards of every shape and form, but at all costs avoid one thing: success. I heard no more from him, and I am not aware that my reply was published with the other testimonials. (LL 10)

———

The greatest need of our time is to clean out the enormous mass of mental and emotional rubbish that clutters our minds and makes all political and social life a mass illness. Without this house cleaning we cannot begin to see. Unless we see, we cannot think. The purification must begin with the mass media. How? (CGB 64)

———

The basic inner moral contradiction of our age is that, though we talk and dream about freedom (or say we dream of it, though I sometimes question that!), though we fight wars over it, our civilization is strictly *servile*. I do not use this term contemptuously, but in its original sense of "pragmatic," oriented exclusively to the useful, making use of means for material ends. The progress of technological culture has in fact been a progress in servility, that is in techniques of *using* material resources, mechanical inventions, etc., in order to get things done. This has, however, two grave disadvantages. First, the notion of the *gratuitous* and the *liberal* (the end in itself) has been lost. Hence we have made ourselves incapable of that happiness which transcends servility and simply rejoices in being for its own sake. Such "liberality" is in fact completely foreign to the technological mentality as we have it now (though not necessarily foreign to it in essence). Second, and inseparable from this, we have in practice developed a completely servile concept of man. Our professed ideals may still pay lip service to the dignity of the person, but without a sense of *being* and a respect for being, there can be no real appreciation of the person. We are so obsessed with *doing* that we have no time and no imagination left for *being*. (CGB 281–282)

THE TECHNOLOGICAL
IMPERATIVE

Science and technology are indeed admirable in many respects, and if they fulfill their promises, they can do much for man. But they can never solve his deepest problems. On the contrary, without wisdom, without the intuition and freedom that enable man to return to the root of his being, science can only precipitate him still further into the centrifugal flight that flings him, in all his compact and uncomprehending isolation, into the darkness of outer space without purpose and without objective.   (FAV 224)

———

Technology can elevate and improve man's life only on one condition: that it remains subservient to his *real* interests; that it respects his true being; that it remembers that the origin and goal of all being is in God. But when technology merely takes over all being for its own purposes, merely exploits and uses up all things in the pursuit of its own ends, and makes everything, including man himself, subservient to its processes, then it degrades man, despoils the world, ravages life, and leads to ruin.   (CGB 230)

It does us no good to make fantastic progress if we do not know how to live with it, if we cannot make good use of it, and if, in fact, our technology becomes nothing more than an expensive and complicated way of cultural disintegration. It is bad form to say such things, to recognize such possibilities. But they are possibilities, and they are not often intelligently taken into account. People get emotional about them from time to time, and then try to sweep them aside into forgetfulness. The fact remains that we have created for ourselves a culture which is not yet livable for mankind as a whole.   (CGB 60)

———

It is precisely the illusion that mechanical progress means human improvement that alienates us from our own being and our own reality. It is precisely because we are convinced that our life, as such, is better if we have a better car, a better TV set, better toothpaste, etc., that we condemn and destroy our own reality and the reality of our natural resources. Technology was made for man, not man for technology. In losing touch with being and thus with God, we have fallen into a senseless idolatry of production and consumption for their own sakes. We have renounced the act of being and plunged ourselves into process for its own sake. We no longer know how to live, and because we cannot accept life in its reality life ceases to be a joy and becomes an affliction. And we even go so far as to blame God for it! The evil in the world is all of our own making, and it proceeds entirely from our ruthless, senseless, wasteful, destructive, and suicidal neglect of our own being.   (CGB 202)

———

I believe the reason for the inner confusion of Western man is that our technological society has no longer any place in it for wisdom that seeks truth for its own sake, that seeks the fullness of being, that seeks to rest in an intuition of the very ground of all being. Without wisdom, the apparent opposition of action and contemplation, work and rest, of involvement and detachment, can never be resolved. Ancient and traditional societies, whether of Asia or of the West, always specifically recognized "the way" of the wise, the way of spiritual discipline in which there was at once wisdom and method, and by which, whether in art, in philosophy, in religion, or in the monastic life, some men would attain to the inner meaning of being, they would experience this meaning for all their brothers, they would so to speak bring together in themselves the divisions or complications that confused the life of their fellows. By healing the divisions in themselves they would help heal the divisions of the whole world. They would realize in themselves that unity which is at the same time the highest action and the purest rest, true knowledge and selfless love, a knowledge beyond knowledge in emptiness and unknowing; a willing beyond will in apparent non-activity. They would attain to the highest striving in the absence of striving and of contention. (FAV 217-218)

EVENTS AND PSEUDO-EVENTS

Nine tenths of the news, as printed in the papers, is pseudo-news, manufactured events. Some days ten tenths. The ritual morning trance, in which one scans columns of newsprint, creates a peculiar form of generalized pseudo-attention to a pseudo-reality. This experience is taken seriously. It is one's daily immersion in "reality." One's orientation to the rest of the world. One's way of reassuring himself that he has not fallen behind. That he is still there. That he still counts!

My own experience has been that renunciation of this self-hypnosis, of this participation in the unquiet universal trance, is no sacrifice of reality at all. To "fall behind" in this sense is to get out of the big cloud of dust that everybody is kicking up, to breathe and to see a little more clearly. (FAV 151)

The things that we do, the things that make our news, the things that are contemporary, are abominations of superstition, of idolatry, proceeding from minds that are full of myths, distortions, half-truths, prejudices, evasions, illusions, in a word—simulacra. Ideas and conceptions that look good but aren't. Ideals that claim to be humane and prove themselves, in their effects, to be callous, cruel, cynical, sometimes even criminal. (FAV 153)

————

Why can we not be content with the secret gift of the happiness that God offers us, without consulting the rest of the world? Why do we insist, rather, on a happiness that is approved by the magazines and TV? Perhaps because we do not believe in a happiness that is given to us for nothing. We do not think we can be happy with a happiness that has no price tag on it. (CGB 84)

————

The real violence exerted by propaganda is this: by means of apparent truth and apparent reason, it induces us to surrender our freedom and self-possession. It predetermines us to certain conclusions, and does so in such a way that we imagine that we are fully free in reaching them by our own judgment and our own thought. Propaganda makes up our minds for us but in such a way that it leaves us the sense of pride and satisfaction of men who have made up their own minds. And, in the last analysis, propaganda achieves this effect because we want it to.

This is one of the few real pleasures left to modern man: this illusion that he is thinking for himself when, in fact, someone else is doing his thinking for him. And this someone else is not a personal authority, the great mind of a genial thinker, it is the mass mind, the general "they," the anonymous whole. One is left, therefore, not only with the sense that one has thought things out for himself, but that he has also reached the correct answer without difficulty—the answer which is shown to be correct because it is the answer of everybody. Since it is at once my answer and the answer of everybody, how should I resist it? (CGB 216–217)

———

I have watched TV twice in my life. I am frankly not terribly interested in TV anyway. Certainly I do not pretend that by simply refusing to keep up with the latest news I am therefore unaffected by what goes on, or free of it all. Certainly events happen and they affect me as they do other people. It is important for me to know about them too: but I refrain from trying to know them in their fresh condition as "news." When they reach me they have become slightly stale. I eat the same tragedies as others, but in the form of tasteless crusts. The news reaches me in the long run through books and magazines, and no longer as a stimulant. Living without news is like living without cigarettes (another peculiarity of the monastic life).

The need for this habitual indulgence quickly disappears. So, when you hear news without the "need" to hear it, it treats you differently. And you treat it differently too. (FAV 151)

———

Today, with the enormous amplification of news and of opinion, we are suffering from more than acceptable distortions of perspective. Our supposed historical consciousness, over-informed and over-stimulated, is threatened with death by bloating, and we are overcome with a political elephantiasis which sometimes seems to make all actual forward motion useless if not impossible. But in addition to the sheer volume of information there is the even more portentous fact of falsification and misinformation by which those in power are often completely intent not only on misleading others but even on convincing themselves that their own lies are "historical truth." (FAV 250)

———

In primitive societies, where men are just beginning to read and having nothing to read but propaganda, we can say that they are its innocent victims. But in an evolved society there are no innocent victims of propaganda. Propaganda succeeds because men want it to succeed. It works on minds because those minds want to be worked on. Its conclusions bring apparent light and satisfaction because that is the kind of satisfaction that people are longing for. It leads them to actions for which they are already half prepared: all they ask is that these actions be justified. If war propaganda succeeds, it is because people want war, and only need a few good reasons to justify their own desire. (CGB 218)

————

How are we to avoid the common obsession with pseudo events in order to construct what seems to us to be a credible idol? It is a nasty question, but it needs to be considered, for in it is contained the mystery of the evil of our time.

I do not have an answer to the question, but I suspect the root of it is this: if we love our own ideology and our own opinion instead of loving our brother, we will seek only to glorify our ideas and our institutions and by that fact we will make real communication impossible. I think Bonhoeffer[4] was absolutely right when he said our real task is to bear in ourselves the fury of the world against Christ in order to reconcile the world with Christ. (FAV 163)

PART THREE

ANTIDOTES TO ILLUSION

Merton believed that our "real selves" had allies in those religious principles and practices that deepened our capacity for humility and compunction. Much of his best writing articulated the transformative power of these essential values.

TRUTH

A sincere man is not so much one who sees the truth and manifests it as he sees it, but one who loves the truth with pure love. (NM 198)

———

Basically our first duty today is to human truth in its existential reality, and this sooner or later brings us into confrontation with system and power which seek to overwhelm truth for the sake of particular interests, perhaps rationalized as ideals. Sooner or later this human duty presents itself in a form of crisis that cannot be evaded. At such a time it is very good, almost essential, to have at one's side others with a similar determination, and one can then be guided by a common inspiration and a communion in truth. Here true strength can be found. A completely isolated witness is much more difficult and dangerous. In the end that too may become necessary. But in any case we know that our only ultimate strength is in the Lord and in His Spirit, and faith must make us depend entirely on His will and providence. One must then truly be detached and free in order not to be held and impeded by anything secondary or irrelevant. Which is another way of saying that poverty also is our strength. (CFT 159)

———

We are living under a tyranny of untruth which confirms itself in power and establishes a more and more total control over men in proportion as they convince themselves they are resisting error.

Our submission to plausible and useful lies involves us in greater and more obvious contradictions, and to hide these from ourselves we need greater and ever less plausible lies. The basic falsehood is the lie that we are totally dedicated to truth, and that we can remain dedicated to truth in a manner that is at the same time honest and exclusive: that we have the monopoly of all truth, just as our adversary of the moment has the monopoly of all error.

We then convince ourselves that we cannot preserve our purity of vision and our inner sincerity if we enter into dialogue with the enemy, for he will corrupt us with 'his error. We believe, finally, that truth cannot be preserved except by the destruction of the enemy—for, since we have identified him with error, to destroy him is to destroy error. The adversary,[5] of course, has exactly the same thoughts about us and exactly the same basic policy by which he defends the "truth." He has identified us with dishonesty, insincerity, and untruth. He believes that, if we are destroyed, nothing will be left but truth. (CGB 56)

———

Our task is not suddenly to burst out into the dazzle of utter unadulterated truth but laboriously to reshape an accurate and honest language that will permit communication between men on all social levels, instead of multiplying a Babel of esoteric and technical tongues which isolate men in their specialties. (LE 272)

———

We make ourselves real by telling the truth. (NM 188)

SILENCE

There is in all visible things an invisible fecundity, a
dimmed light, a meek namelessness, a hidden whole-
ness. This mysterious Unity and Integrity is Wisdom,
the Mother of all, *Natura naturans.*[6] There is in all
things an inexhaustible sweetness and purity, a silence
that is a fount of action and joy. It rises up in wordless
gentleness and flows out to me from the unseen roots
of all created being, welcoming me tenderly, saluting
me with indescribable humility. This is at once my own
being, my own nature, and the Gift of my Creator's
Thought and Art within me, speaking as *Hagia Sophia*,[7]
speaking as my sister, Wisdom. (CP 363)

———

Those who love their own noise are impatient of everything else. They constantly defile the silence of
the forests and the mountains and the sea. They bore
through silent nature in every direction with their
machines, for fear that the calm world might accuse
them of their own emptiness. The urgency of their
swift movement seems to ignore the tranquility of nature by pretending to have a purpose. The loud plane

seems for a moment to deny the reality of the clouds and of the sky, by its direction, its noise, and its pretended strength. The silence of the sky remains when the plane has gone. The tranquility of the clouds will remain when the plane has fallen apart. It is the silence of the world that is real. Our noise, our business, our purposes, and all our fatuous statements about our purposes, our business, and our noise: these are the illusion. (NM 257)

———

The deepest level of communication is not communication, but communion. It is wordless. It is beyond words. It is beyond speech, and it is beyond concept. Not that we discover a new unity. We discover an older unity. My dear Brothers, we are already one. But we imagine that we are not. And what we have to recover is our original unity. What we have to be is what we are. (AJ 308)

SOLITUDE

Ours is certainly a time for solitaries and hermits. But merely to reproduce the simplicity, austerity, and prayer of these primitive souls is not a complete or satisfactory answer. We must transcend them, and liberate ourselves in our own way, from involvement in a world that is plunging to disaster. But our world is different from theirs. Our involvement in it is more complete. Our danger is far more desperate. (WOD 23)

––––––––––

You will never find interior solitude unless you make some conscious effort to deliver yourself from the desires and the cares and the attachments of an existence in time and in the world.

Do everything you can to avoid the noise and the business of men. Keep as far away as you can from the places where they gather to cheat and insult one another, to exploit one another, to laugh at one another, or to mock one another with their false gestures of friendship. Be glad if you can keep beyond the reach of their radios. Do not bother with their unearthly songs. Do not read their advertisements.

The contemplative life certainly does not demand a self-righteous contempt for the habits and diversions of ordinary people. But nevertheless, no man who seeks liberation and light in solitude, no man who seeks spiritual freedom, can afford to yield passively to all the appeals of a society of salesmen, advertisers and consumers. There is no doubt that life cannot be lived on a human level without certain legitimate pleasures. But to say that all the pleasures which offer themselves to us as necessities are now "legitimate" is quite another story. A natural pleasure is one thing; an unnatural pleasure, forced upon the satiated mind by the importunity of a salesman is quite another. (NS 84–85)

––––––––

Keep your eyes clean and your ears quiet and your mind serene. Breathe God's air. Work, if you can, under His sky. But if you have to live in a city and work among machines and ride in the subways and eat in a place where the radio makes you deaf with spurious news and where the food destroys your life and the sentiments of those around you poison your heart with boredom, do not be impatient, but accept it as the love of God and as a seed of solitude planted in your soul. If you are appalled by those things, you will keep your appetite for the healing silence of recollection. But meanwhile—keep your sense of compassion for the men who have forgotten the very concept of solitude. You, at least, know that it exists, and that it is the source of peace and joy. You can still hope for such joy. They do not even hope for it any more. (NS 86–87)

———

I ought to know, by now, that God uses everything that happens as a means to lead me into solitude. Every creature that enters my life, every instant of my days, will be designed to wound me with the realization of the world's insufficiency, until I become so detached that I will be able to find God alone in everything. Only then will all things bring me joy. (SOJ 51)

———

Do you think the way to sanctity is to lock yourself up with your prayers and your books and the meditations that please and interest your mind, to protect yourself with many walls, against people you consider stupid? Do you think the way to contemplation is found in the refusal of activities and works which are necessary for the good of others but which happen to bore and distract you? Do you imagine that you will discover God by winding yourself up in a cocoon of spiritual and aesthetic pleasures, instead of renouncing all your tastes and desires and ambitions and satisfactions for the love of Christ, Who will not even live within you if you cannot find Him in other men? (NS 191–192)

———

People are constantly trying to use you to help them create the particular illusions by which they live. This is particularly true of the collective illusions which sometimes are accepted *as* ideologies. You must renounce and sacrifice the approval that is only a bribe enlisting your support of a collective illusion. You must not allow yourself to be represented as some one in whom a few of the favorite daydreams of the public have come true. You must be willing, if necessary, to become a disturbing and therefore an undesired person, one who is not wanted because he upsets the general dream. But be careful that you do not do this in the service of some other dream that is only a little less general and therefore seems to you the more real because it is more exclusive! (CGB 83)

———

This is what it means to seek God perfectly: to withdraw from illusion and pleasure, from worldly anxieties and desires, from the works that God does not want, from a glory that is only human display; to keep my mind free from confusion in order that my liberty may be always at the disposal of His will; to entertain silence in my heart and listen for the voice of God; to cultivate an intellectual freedom from the images of created things in order to receive the secret contact of God in obscure love;

to love all men as myself; to rest in humility and to find peace in withdrawal from conflict and competition with other men; to turn aside from controversy and put away heavy loads of judgment and censorship and criticism and the whole burden of opinions that I have no obligation to carry; to have a will that is always ready to fold back within itself and draw all the powers of the soul down from its deepest center to rest in silent expectancy for the coming of God, poised in tranquil and effortless concentration *upon* the point of my dependence on Him; to gather all that I am, and have all that I can possibly suffer or do or be, and abandon them all to God in the resignation of a perfect love and blind faith and pure trust in God, to do His will. (NS 45–46)

———

The true solitary does not have to run away from others: they cease to notice him, because he does not share their love for an illusion. The soul that is truly solitary becomes perfectly colorless and ceases to excite either the love or the hatred of others by reason of its solitude. The true solitary can, no doubt, become a hated and a hunted person: but not by reason of anything that is in himself. He will only be hated if he has a divine work to do in the world. For his work will bring him into conflict with the world. His solitude, as such, creates no such conflict. Solitude brings persecution only when it takes the form of a "mission," and then there is something much more in it than solitude. For when the solitary finds that his solitude has taken on the character of a mission, he discovers that he has become a force that reacts on the very heart of the society in which he lives, a power that disturbs and impedes and accuses the forces of selfishness and pride, reminding others of their own need for solitude and for charity and for peace with God. (NM 252)

———

The world is the unquiet city of those who live for themselves and are therefore divided against one another in a struggle that cannot end, for it will go on eternally in hell. It is the city of those who are fighting for possession of limited things and for the monopoly of goods and pleasures that cannot be shared by all.

But if you try to escape from this world merely by leaving the city and hiding yourself in solitude, you will only take the city with you into solitude. For the flight from the world is nothing else but the flight from self-concern. And the man who locks himself up in private with his own selfishness has put himself into a position where the evil within him will either possess him like a devil or drive him out of his head.

That is why it is dangerous to go into solitude merely because you like to be alone. (NS 78–79)

PRAYER, MEDITATION, CONTEMPLATION

If we really want prayer, we'll have to give it time. We must slow down to a human tempo and we'll begin to have time to listen. And as soon as we listen to what's going on, things will begin to take shape by themselves. (CNP 56)

———

It is a risky thing to pray, and the danger is that our very prayers get between God and us. The great thing in prayer is not to pray, but to go directly to God. If saying your prayers is an obstacle to prayer, cut it out. Let Jesus pray. Thank God Jesus is praying. Forget yourself. Enter into the prayer of Jesus. Let him pray in you.

The best way to pray is: stop. Let prayer pray within you, whether you know it or not. This means a deep awareness of your true inner identity. There are no levels. Any moment you can break through into the underlying unity which is God's gift in Christ. In this end, Praise praises. Thanksgiving gives thanks. Jesus prays. Openness is all. (CNP 57)

All prayer, reading, meditation and all the activities of the monastic life are aimed at *purity of heart,* an unconditional and totally humble surrender to God, a total acceptance of ourselves and of our situation as willed by him. It means the renunciation of all deluded images of ourselves, all exaggerated estimates of our own capacities, in order to obey God's will as it comes to us in the difficult demands of life in its exacting truth. *Purity of heart* is then correlative to a new spiritual identity—the "self" as recognized in the context of realities willed by God—Purity of heart is the enlightened awareness of the new man, as opposed to the complex and perhaps rather disreputable fantasies of the "old man."

Meditation is then ordered to this new insight, this direct knowledge of the self in its higher aspect. (CTP 68)

———

The great thing is prayer. Prayer itself. If you want a life of prayer, the way to get it is by praying. We were indoctrinated so much into means and ends that we don't realize that there is a different dimension in the life of prayer. In technology you have this horizontal progress, where you must start at one point and move to another and then another. But that is not the way to build a life of prayer. In prayer we discover what we already have. You start where you are and you deepen what you already have. And you realize that you are already there. (CNP 56–57)

———

If you have never had any distractions, you don't know how to pray. For the secret of prayer is a hunger for God and for the vision of God, a hunger that lies far deeper than the level of language or affection. And a man whose memory and imagination are persecuting him with a crowd of useless or even evil thoughts and images may sometimes be forced to pray far better, in the depths of his murdered heart, than one whose mind is swimming with clear concepts and brilliant purposes and easy acts of love. (NS 221–222)

———

Finally, the purest prayer is something on which it is impossible to reflect until after it is over. And when the grace has gone we no longer seek to reflect on it, because we realize that it belongs to another order of things, and that it will be in some sense debased by our reflecting on it. Such prayer desires no witness, even the witness of our own souls. It seeks to keep itself entirely hidden in God. The experience remains in our spirit like a wound, like a scar that will not heal. But we do not reflect upon it. This living wound may become a source of knowledge, if we are to instruct others in the ways of prayer; or else it may become a bar and an obstacle to knowledge, a seal of silence set upon the soul, closing the way to words and thoughts, so that we can say nothing of it to other men. (NM 50–51)

———

Meditation is almost all contained in this one idea: the idea of awakening our interior self and attuning ourselves inwardly to the Holy Spirit, so that we will be able to respond to His grace. In mental prayer, over the years, we must allow our interior perceptivity to be refined and purified. We must attune ourselves to unexpected movements of grace, which do not fit our own preconceived ideas of the spiritual life at all, and which in no way flatter our own ambitious aspirations.

We must be ready to co-operate not only with graces that console, but with graces that humiliate us. Not only with lights that exalt us, but with lights that blast our self-complacency. Much of our coldness and dryness in prayer may well be a kind of unconscious defense against grace. Without realizing it, we allow our nature to desensitize our souls so that we cannot perceive graces which we intuitively foresee may prove to be painful.

Meditation is then always to be associated in practice with abandonment to the will and action of God. It goes hand in hand with self-renunciation and with obedience to the Holy Spirit. Meditation that does not seek to bring our whole being into conformity with God's will must naturally remain sterile and abstract. But any sincere interior prayer that really seeks this one all important end—our conformity to God's will in our regard—cannot fail to be rewarded by grace. It will prove, without question, to be one of the most sanctifying forces in our lives. And St Teresa of Avila believed that no one who was faithful to the practice of meditation could possibly lose his soul. (SD&M 85–86)

———

If well made, my meditation will bear fruit in an increase of fortitude in patience. My patience will help me endure trials in such a way that my soul will be purified of many imperfections and obstacles to grace. I will learn to know better the sources of anger in myself. I will then grow in charity. (SD&M 59)

———

What we need is not a false peace which enables us to evade the implacable light of judgment, but the grace courageously to accept the bitter truth that is revealed to us; to abandon our inertia, our egoism and submit entirely to the demands of the Spirit, praying earnestly for help, and giving ourselves generously to *every effort asked of* us *by God.* (CTP 103–104)

Even the capacity to recognize our condition before
God is itself a grace. We cannot always attain it at will.
To learn meditation does not mean learning an artificial
technique for infallibly producing "compunction" and
the "sense of our nothingness" whenever we please. On
the contrary, this would be the result of violence and
would be inauthentic. Meditation implies the capacity
to *receive* this grace whenever God wishes to grant it
to us, and therefore a permanent disposition to humility, attention to reality, receptivity, pliability. To learn
to meditate then means to gradually get free from habitual hardness of heart, torpor and grossness of mind,
due to arrogance and non-acceptance of simple reality, or resistance to the concrete demands of God's
will. (CTP 71)

The most usual entrance to contemplation is through
a desert of aridity in which, although you see nothing
and feel nothing and apprehend nothing and are conscious only of a certain interior suffering and anxiety,
yet you are drawn and held in this darkness and dryness because it is the only place in which you can find
any kind of stability and peace. As you progress, you
learn to rest in this arid quietude, and the assurance

of a comforting and mighty presence at the heart of this experience grows on you more and more, until you gradually realize that it is God revealing Himself to you in a light that is painful to your nature and to all its faculties, because it is infinitely above them and because its purity is at war with your own selfishness and darkness and imperfection. (NM 275–276)

———

Contemplative prayer is, in a way, simply the preference for the desert, for emptiness, for poverty. One has begun to know the meaning of contemplation when he intuitively and spontaneously seeks the dark and unknown path/of aridity in preference to every other way. The contemplative is one who would rather not know than know. Rather not enjoy than enjoy. Rather not have *proof* that God loves him. He accepts the love of God on faith, in defiance of all apparent evidence. This is the necessary condition, and a very paradoxical condition, for the mystical experience of the reality of God's presence and of his love for us. Only when we are able to "let go" of everything within all desire to see, to know, to taste and to experience the presence of God, do we truly become able to experience that presence with the overwhelming conviction and reality that revolutionize our entire inner life. (CTP 89)

———

The contemplative life isn't something objective that is "there" and to which, after fumbling around, you finally gain access. The contemplative life is a dimension of our subjective existence. Discovering the contemplative life is a new self-discovery. One might say it is the flowering of a deeper identity on an entirely different plane from a mere psychological discovery, a paradoxical new identity that is found only in loss of self. To find one's self by losing one's self: that is part of "contemplation." Remember the Gospel, "He who would save his life must lose it?"[8] (CIWA 340)

————

The contemplative way is in no sense a deliberate "technique" of self-emptying in order to produce an esoteric experience. It is the paradoxical response to an almost incomprehensible call from God, drawing us into solitude, plunging us into darkness and silence, not to withdraw and protect us from peril, but to bring us safely through untold dangers by a miracle of love and power. The contemplative way is, in fact, not a way. Christ alone is the way, and he is invisible. The "desert" of contemplation is simply a metaphor to explain the state of emptiness which we experience when we have left all ways, forgotten ourselves and taken the invisible Christ as our way. (CTP 92)

————

The contemplative life must provide an area, a space of liberty, of silence, in which possibilities are allowed to surface and new choices—beyond routine choice—become manifest. It should create a new experience of time, not as stopgap, stillness, but as "temps vierge"[9]—not a blank to be filled or an untouched; space to be conquered and violated, but a space which can enjoy its own potentialities and hopes—and its own presence to itself. One's *own* time. But not dominated by one's own ego and its demands. Hence open to *others*—*compassionate* time, rooted in the sense of common illusion and in criticism of it. (AJ 117)

———————

The way to contemplation is an obscurity so obscure that it is no longer even dramatic. There is nothing in it that can be grasped and cherished as heroic or even unusual. And so, for a contemplative, there is supreme value in the ordinary everyday routine of work, poverty, hardship and monotony that characterize the lives of all the poor, uninteresting and forgotten people in the world . . . The surest ascetism is the bitter insecurity and labor and nonentity of the really poor. To be utterly dependent on other people. To be ignored and despised and forgotten. To know little of respectability or comfort. To take orders and work hard for little or no money: it is a hard school, and one which most pious people do their best to avoid.

No one teaches contemplation except God, Who gives it. The best you can do is write something or say something that will serve as an occasion for someone else to realize what God wants of him. (NS 250)

————

The contemplative life has nothing to tell you except to reassure you and say that if you dare to penetrate your own silence and dare to advance without fear into the solitude of your own heart and risk the sharing of that solitude with the lonely other who seeks God through you and with you, then you will truly recover the light and the capacity to understand what is beyond words and beyond explanations because it is too close to be explained: it is the intimate union in the depths of your heart, of God's spirit and your own innermost self, so that you and He are in truth One Spirit. (MJ 173)

MONASTICISM

The monastic life is in a certain sense scandalous. The monk is precisely a *man who has* no *specific task.* He is liberated from the routines and servitudes of organized human activity in order to *be free.* Free for what? Free to see, free to praise, free to understand, free to love. This ideal is easy to describe, much more difficult to realize. Obviously, in reality, the life of a monastic community has many tasks and even certain organized routines so that the monk, in his own little world, lives a social life like everybody else. This social life can become complicated and overactive. And he suffers the same temptations to evasion, to meaninglessness, to bad faith, to restless agitation. But the purpose of the monastic life is to enable a man to face reality in all its naked, disconcerting, possibly drab and disappointing factuality, without excuses, without useless explanations, and without subterfuges. (CIWA 228)

———

The monk is not defined by his task, his usefulness. In a certain sense he is supposed to be "useless" because his mission is not to *do* this or that job but to *be* a man of God. He does not live in order to exercise a specific function: his business is life itself. This means that monasticism aims at the cultivation of a certain *quality* of life, a level of awareness, a depth of consciousness, an area of transcendence and of adoration which are not usually possible in an active secular existence. This does not imply that the secular level is entirely godless and reprobate, or that there can be no real awareness of God in the world. Nor does it mean that worldly life is to be considered wicked or even inferior. But it does mean that more immersion and total absorption in worldly business end by robbing one of a certain necessary perspective. The monk seeks to be free from what William Faulkner called "the same frantic steeplechase toward nothing" which is the essence of "worldliness" everywhere. (CIWA 7)

———

An abbey is an earthly paradise because it is an earthly purgatory. (SJ 186)

———

We are living through the greatest crisis in the history of man; and this crisis is centered precisely in the country that has made a fetish out of action and has lost (or perhaps never had) the sense of contemplation. Far from being irrelevant, prayer, meditation and contemplation are of the utmost importance in

America today. Unfortunately, it must be admitted that the official contemplative life as it is lived in our monasteries needs a great deal of rethinking, because it is still too closely identified with patterns of thought that were accepted five hundred years ago, but which are completely strange to modern man. (CIWA 164)

———

The whole illusion of a separate holy existence is a dream. Not that I question the reality of vocation, or my monastic life: but the conception of "separation from the world" that we have in the monastery too easily presents itself as a complete illusion: the illusion that by making vows we become a different species of being, pseudo-angels, "spiritual men," men of interior life, what have you . . . Thank God, thank God that I am like other men, that I am only a man among others. (CGB 140–141)

———

If there is a "problem" for Christianity today, it is the problem of the identification of "Christendom" with certain forms of culture and society, certain political and social structures which for fifteen-hundred years have dominated Europe and the West. The first monks were men who, already in the fourth century, began to protest against this identification as a falsehood and a servitude. Fifteen-hundred years of European Christendom, in spite of certain definite achievements, have not been an unequivocal glory for Christendom. The time has come for judgment to be passed on this history. I can rejoice in this fact, believing that the judgment will be a liberation of the Christian faith from servitude to and involvement in the structures of the secular world. And that is why I think certain forms of Christian "optimism" are to be taken with reservations, in so far as they lack the genuine eschatological consciousness of the Christian vision, and concentrate upon the naive hope of merely temporal achievements—churches on the moon. (HR 66)

FAITH

The man who does not permit his spirit to be beaten down and upset by dryness and helplessness, but who lets God lead him peacefully through the wilderness, and desires no other support or guidance than that of pure faith and trust in God alone, will be brought to the Promised Land. (NS 239)

––––––––

Absurdity is the anguish of realizing that underneath the apparently logical pattern of a more or less "well organized" and rational life, there lies an abyss of irrationality, confusion, pointlessness, and indeed of apparent chaos. This is what immediately impresses itself upon the man who has renounced diversion. It cannot be otherwise; for in renouncing diversion, he renounces the seemingly harmless pleasure of building a tight, self-contained illusion about himself and his little world. He accepts the difficulty of facing the million things in his life which are incomprehensible instead of simply ignoring them. Incidentally it is only when the apparent absurdity of life is faced in all truth that faith really becomes possible. Otherwise, faith tends to be a kind of diversion, a spiritual amusement, in which one gathers up accepted, conventional formulas and arranges them in the approved mental patterns, without bothering to investigate their meaning, or asking if they have any practical consequences in one's life. (DQ 179–180)

––––––––

Self-confidence is a precious natural gift, a sign of health. But it is not the same thing as faith. Faith is much deeper, and it must be deep enough to subsist when we are weak, when we are sick, when our self-confidence is gone, when our self-respect is gone. I do not mean that faith *only* functions when we are otherwise in a state of collapse. But true faith must be able to go on even when everything else is taken away from us. Only a humble man is able to accept faith on these terms, so completely without reservation that he is glad of it in its pure state, and welcomes it happily even when nothing else comes with it, and when everything else is taken away. (NS 187)

––––––––

How many people there are in the world of today who have "lost their faith" along with the vain hopes and illusions of their childhood. What they called "faith" was just one among all the other illusions. They placed all their hope in a certain sense of spiritual peace, of comfort, of interior equilibrium, of self-respect. Then when they began to struggle with the real difficulties and burdens of mature life, when they became aware of their own weakness, they lost their peace, they let go of their precious self-respect, and it became impossible for them to "believe." That is to say it became impossible for them to comfort themselves, to reassure themselves, with the images and concepts that they found reassuring in childhood. Place no hope in the feeling of assurance, in spiritual comfort. You may well have to get along without this. (NS 186–187)

––––––

Indeed, the truth that many people never understand, until it is too late, is that the more you try to avoid suffering, the more you suffer, because smaller and more insignificant things begin to torture you, in proportion to your fear of being hurt. The one who does most to avoid suffering is, in the end, the one who suffers most: and his suffering comes to him from things so little and so trivial that one can say that it is no longer objective at all. It is his own existence, his own being, that is at once the subject and the source of his pain, and his very existence and consciousness is his greatest torture. This is another of the great perversions by which the devil uses our philosophies to turn our whole nature inside out, and eviscerate all our capacities for good, turning them against ourselves. (SSM 82–83)

In getting the best of our secret attachments—ones which we cannot see because they are principles of spiritual blindness—our own initiative is almost always useless. We need to leave the initiative in the hands of God working in our souls either directly in the night of aridity and suffering, or through events and other men.

This is where so many holy people break down and go to pieces. As soon as they reach the point where they can no longer see the way and guide themselves by their own light, they refuse to go any further. They have no confidence in anyone except themselves. Their faith is largely an emotional illusion. It is rooted in their feelings, in their physique, in their temperament. It is a kind of natural optimism that is stimulated by moral activity and warmed by the approval of other men. If people oppose it, this kind of faith still finds refuge in self-complacency. But when the time comes to enter the darkness in which we are naked and helpless and alone; in which we see the insufficiency of our greatest strength and the hollowness of our strongest virtues; in which we have nothing of our own to rely on, and nothing in our nature to support us, and nothing in the world to guide us or give us light—then we find out whether or not we live by faith. It is in this darkness, when there is nothing left in us that can please or comfort our own minds, when we seem to be useless and worthy of all contempt, when we seem to have failed, when we seem to be destroyed and devoured, it is then that the deep and secret selfishness that is too close for us to identify is stripped away from our souls. It is in this darkness that we find true liberty. It is in this abandonment that we are made strong. This is the night which empties us and makes us pure. (NS 257–258)

————

Faith then is not just the grim determination to cling to a certain form of words, no matter what may happen—though we must certainly be prepared to defend our creed with our life. But above all faith is the opening of the inward eye, the eye of the heart, to be filled with the presence of the Divine light. (NS 129–130)

————

If we are not humble, we tend to demand that faith must also bring with it good health, peace of mind, good luck, success in business, popularity, world peace, and every other good thing we can imagine. And it is true that God can give us all these good things if He wants to. But they are of no importance compared with faith, which is essential. If we insist on other things as the price of our believing, we tend by that very fact to undermine our own belief. I do not think it would be an act of mercy on God's part simply to let us get away with this! (NS 187–188)

———————

Be careful of every vain hope: it is in reality a temptation to despair. It may seem very real, very substantial. You may come to depend far too much on this apparent solidity of what you think is soon to be yours. You may make your whole spiritual life, your very faith itself, depend on this illusory promise. Then, when it dissolves into air, everything else dissolves along with it. Your whole spiritual life slips away between your fingers and you are left with nothing.

In reality, this could be a good thing, and we should be able to regard it as a good thing, if only we could fall back on the substantiality of pure and obscure faith, which cannot deceive us. But our faith is weak. Indeed, too often the weakest thing about our faith is the illusion that our faith is strong, when the "strength" we feel is only the intensity of emotion or of sentiment, which has nothing to do with real faith. (NS 186)

CHARITY

Charity is a love for God which respects the need that other men have for Him. Therefore, charity alone can give us the power and the delicacy to love others without defiling their loneliness which is their need and their salvation. (NM 244)

———

This is the great paradox of charity: that unless we are selfish enough to desire to become perfectly unselfish, we have not charity. And unless we love ourselves enough to seek perfect happiness in the total forgetfulness of ourselves, we will never find happiness. Charity is a self-interest which seeks fulfillment in the renunciation of all its interests. (BIW 102)

———

It is easy enough to tell the poor to accept their poverty as God's will when you yourself have warm clothes and plenty of food and medical care and a roof over your head and no worry about the rent. But if you want them to believe you—try to share some of their poverty and see if you accept it as God's will yourself! (NS 179)

HUMILITY

The value of our activity depends almost entirely on the humility to accept ourselves as we are. The reason why we do things so badly is that we are not content to do what we can. We insist on doing what is not asked of us, because we want to taste the success that belongs to somebody else. We never discover what it is like to make a success of our own work, because we do not want to undertake *any* work that is merely proportionate to our powers. Who is willing to be satisfied with a job that expresses all his limitations? He will accept such work only as a "means of livelihood" while he waits to discover his "true vocation." The world is full of unsuccessful businessmen who still secretly believe they were meant to be artists or writers or actors in the movies. (NM 124)

———

We cannot avoid missing the point of almost everything we do. But what of it? Life is not a matter of getting something out of everything. Life itself is imperfect. All created beings begin to die as soon as they begin to live and no one expects any one of them to become absolutely perfect, still less to stay that way. Each individual thing is only a sketch of the specific perfection planned for its kind. Why should we ask it to be anything more?

If we are too anxious to find absolute perfection in created things we cease to look for perfection where alone it can be found: in God. The secret of the imperfection of all things, of their inconstancy, their fragility, their falling into nothingness, is that they are only a shadowy expression of the one Being from Whom they receive their being. If they were absolutely perfect and changeless in themselves, they would fail in their vocation, which is to give glory to God by their contingency. (NM 128–129)

————

One who is content with what he has, and who accepts the fact that he inevitably misses very much in life, is far better off than one who has much more but who worries about all he may be missing. For we cannot make the best of what we are, if our hearts are always divided between what we are and what we are not. We cannot be happy if we expect to live all the time at the highest peak of intensity. Happiness is not a matter of intensity but of balance and order and rhythm and harmony. Let us, therefore, learn to pass from one imperfect activity to another without worrying too much about what we are missing. (NM 127–128)

When one has too many answers, and when one joins a chorus of others chanting the same slogans, there is, it seems to me, a danger that one is trying to evade the loneliness of a conscience that realizes itself to be in an inescapably evil situation. We are all under judgment. None of us is free from contamination. Our choice is not that of being pure and whole at the mere cost of formulating a just and honest opinion. Mere commitment to a decent program of action does not lift the curse. Our real choice is between being like Job, who knew he was stricken, and Job's friends who did not know that they were stricken too—though less obvious than he. (So they had answers!) (FAV 145–146)

The fruitfulness of our life depends in large measure on our ability to doubt our own words and to question the value of our own work. The man who completely trusts his own estimate of himself is doomed to sterility. All he asks of any act he performs is that it be *his* act. If it is performed by him, it must be good. All words spoken by him must be infallible. The car he has just bought is the best for its price, for no other reason than that he is the one who has bought it. He seeks no other fruit than this, and therefore he generally gets no other.

If we believe ourselves in part, we may be right about ourselves. If we are completely taken in by our own disguise, we cannot help being wrong. (NM 124–125)

What we need is the gift of God which makes us able to find in ourselves, not just ourselves but Him, and then our nothingness becomes His all. This is not possible without the liberation effected by compunction and humility. It requires not talent, not mere insight, but sorrow, pouring itself out in love and trust. (CQR 214)

Despair is the absolute extreme of self-love. It is reached when a man deliberately turns his back on all help from anyone else in order to taste the rotten luxury of knowing himself to be lost.

In every man there is hidden some root of despair because in every man there is pride that vegetates and springs weeds and rank flowers of self-pity as soon as our own resources fail us. But because our own resources inevitably fail us, we are all more or less subject to discouragement and to despair.

Despair is the ultimate development of a pride so great and so stiff-necked that it selects the absolute misery of damnation rather than accept happiness from the hands of God and thereby acknowledge that He is above us and that we are not capable of fulfilling our destiny by ourselves.

But a man who is truly humble cannot despair, because in the humble man there is no longer any such thing as self-pity. (NS 180)

———

Only the man who has had to face despair is really convinced that he needs mercy. Those who do not want mercy never seek it. It is better to find God on the threshold of despair than to risk our lives in a complacency that has never felt the need of forgiveness. A life that is without problems may literally be more hopeless than one that always verges on despair. (NM 21–22)

———

God is more glorified by a man who uses the good things of this life in simplicity and with gratitude than by the nervous asceticism of someone who is agitated about every detail of his self-denial. The former uses good things and thinks of God. The latter is afraid of good things, and consequently cannot use them properly. He is terrified of the pleasure God has put in things, and in his terror thinks only of himself. He imagines God has placed all the good things of the world before him like bait in a trap. He worries at all times about his own "perfection." His struggle for perfection becomes a kind of battle of wits with the Creator who made all things good. The very goodness of creatures becomes a threat to the purity of this virtuous one, who would like to abstain from everything. But he cannot. He is human, like the rest of men, and must make use like them of food and drink and sleep. Like them he must see the sky, and love, in spite of oneself, the light of the sun! Every feeling of pleasure fills him with a sense of guilt. It has besmirched his own adored perfection. Strange that people like this should enter monasteries which have no other reason for existing than the love of God! (NM 114–115)

———

We must never overlook the fact that the message of the Bible is above all a message preached to the poor, the burdened, the oppressed, the underprivileged. (OTB 51)

———

Asceticism is utterly useless if it turns us into freaks. Pride makes us artificial, and humility makes us real. (NM 113)

———

If you were truly humble you would not bother about yourself at all. Why should you? You would only be concerned with God and with His will and with the objective order of things and values as they are, and not as your selfishness wants them to be. Consequently you would have no more illusions to defend. Your movements would be free. You would not need to be hampered with excuses which are really only framed to defend you against the accusation of pride—as if your humility depended on what other people thought of you! (NS 189–190)

––––––––

A humble man can do great things with an uncommon perfection because he is no longer concerned about incidentals, like his own interests and his own reputation, and therefore he no longer needs to waste his efforts in defending them.

For a humble man is not afraid of failure. In fact, he is not afraid of anything, even of himself, since perfect humility implies perfect confidence in the power of God before Whom no other power has any meaning and for Whom there is no such thing as an obstacle.

Humility is the surest sign of strength. (NS 190)

––––––––

Teach me to bear a humility which shows me, without ceasing, that I am a liar and a fraud and that, even though this is so, I have an obligation to strive after truth, to be as true as I can, even though I will inevitably find all my truth half poisoned with deceit.

This is the terrible thing about humility: that it is never fully successful. If it were only possible to be completely humble on this earth. But no, that is the trouble: You, Lord, were humble. But our humility consists in being proud and knowing all about it, and being crushed by the unbearable weight of it, and to be able to do so little about it.

How stern You are in Your mercy, and yet You must be. Your mercy has to be just because Your Truth has to be True. How stern You are, nevertheless, in Your mercy: for the more we struggle to be true, the more we discover our falsity. Is it merciful of Your light to bring us, inexorably, to despair?

No—it is not to despair that You bring me but to humility. For true humility is, in a way, a very real despair: despair of myself, in order that I may hope entirely in You.

What man can bear to fall into such darkness? (TIS 66)

VOCATION

There is only one vocation. Whether you teach or live in the cloister or nurse the sick, whether you are in religion or out of it, married or single, no matter who you are or what you are, you are called to the summit of perfection: you are called to a deep interior life perhaps even to mystical prayer, and to pass the fruits of your contemplation on to others. And if you cannot do so by word, then by example. (SSM 419)

The fulfillment of every individual vocation demands not only the renouncement of what is evil in itself, but also *of all the precise goods that are not willed for us by God.* It takes exceptional courage and integrity to make such a sacrifice. We cannot do it unless we are really seeking to do the will of God for His sake alone. The man who is content to keep from disobeying God, and to satisfy his own desires wherever there is nothing to prevent him from doing so, may indeed lead a life that is not evil: but his life will remain a sad confusion of truth and falsity and he will never have the spiritual vision to tell one clearly from the other. He will never fully live up to his vocation. (NM 137)

The remarkable thing about St. Francis is that in his sacrifice of everything he had also sacrificed all the "vocations" in a limited sense of the word. After having been edified for centuries by all the various branches of the Franciscan religious family, we are surprised to think that St. Francis started out on the roads of Umbria without the slightest idea that he had a "Franciscan vocation." And in fact he did not. He had thrown all vocations to the winds together with his clothes and other possessions. He did not think of himself as an apostle, but as a tramp. He certainly did not look upon himself as a monk: if he had wanted to be a monk, he would have found plenty of monasteries to enter. He evidently did not go around conscious of the fact that he was a "contemplative." Nor was he worried by comparisons between the active and contemplative lives. Yet he led both at the same time, and with the highest perfection. No good work was alien to him—no work of mercy, whether corporal or spiritual, that did not have a place in his beautiful life! His freedom embraced every thing. (NM 161)

————

Our vocation is not simply to *be*, but to work together with God in the creation of our own life, our own identity, our own destiny. We are free beings and sons of God. This means to say that we should not passively exist, but actively participate in His creative freedom, in our own lives, and in the lives of others, by choosing the truth. To put it better, we are even called to share with God the work of *creating* the truth of our identity.

We can evade this responsibility by playing with masks, and this pleases us because it can appear at times to be a free and creative way of living. It is quite easy, it seems to please everyone. But in the long run the cost and the sorrow come very high. To work out our own identity in God, which the Bible calls "working out our salvation," is a labor that requires sacrifice and anguish, risk and many tears. It demands close attention to reality at every moment, and great fidelity to God as He reveals Himself, obscurely, in the mystery of each new situation. (NS 32)

––––––––

Gratitude and confidence and freedom from ourselves: these are signs that we have found our vocation and are living up to it even though everything else may seem to have gone wrong. They give us peace in any suffering. They teach us to laugh at despair. And we may have to. (NM 140)

GOD

At the center of our being is a point of nothingness which is untouched by sin and by illusion, a point of pure truth, a point or spark which belongs entirely to God, which is never at our disposal, from which God disposes of our lives, which is inaccessible to the fantasies of our own mind or the brutalities of our own will. This little point of nothingness and of *absolute poverty* is the pure glory of God in us. It is so to speak His name written in us, as our poverty, as our indigence, as our dependence, as our sonship. It is like a pure diamond, blazing with the invisible light of heaven. It is in everybody, and if we could see it we would see these billions of points of light coming together in the face and blaze of a sun that would make all the darkness and cruelty of life vanish completely. I have no program for this seeing. It is only given. But the gate of heaven is everywhere. (CGB 142)

———————

In order to find God in ourselves, we must stop looking at ourselves, stop checking and verifying ourselves in the mirror of our own futility, and be content to *be* in Him and to do whatever He wills, according to our limitations, judging our acts not in the light of our own illusions, but in the light of His reality which is all around us in the things and people we live with. (NM 120)

———

We must be saved from immersion in the sea of lies and passions which is called "the world." And we must be saved above all from that abyss of confusion and absurdity which is our own worldly self. The person must be rescued from the individual. The free son of God must be saved from the conformist slave of fantasy, passion and convention. The creative and mysterious inner self must be delivered from the wasteful, hedonistic and destructive ego that seeks only to cover itself with disguises. To be "lost" is to be left to the arbitrariness and pretenses of the contingent ego, the smoke-self that must inevitably vanish. To be "saved" is to return to one's inviolate and eternal reality and to live in God. (NS 38)

———

If we ask the Bible, as we ultimately must when we enter into serious dialog with it: "Who is this Father? What is meant by Father? Show us the Father?" We in our turn are asked in effect: "Who are *you* who seek to know 'the Father' and what do you think you are seeking anyway?" And we are told: Find yourself in love of your brother as if he were Christ (since in fact he 'is Christ') and you will know the Father (see John 14:8–17). That is to say: if you live for *others* you will have an intimate personal knowledge of the love that rises up in you out of a ground that lies beyond your own freedom and your own inclination, and yet is present as the very core of your own free and personal identity. Penetrating to that inner ground of love you at last find your true self. (OTB 33)

————

Fickleness and indecision are signs of self-love. If you can never make up your mind what God wills for you, but are always veering from one opinion to another, from one practice to another, from one method to another, it may be an indication that you are trying to get around God's will and do your own with a quiet conscience.

As soon as God gets you in one monastery you want to be in another.

As soon as you taste one way of prayer, you want to try another. You are always making resolutions and breaking them by counter resolutions. You ask your confessor and do not remember the answers. Before you finish one book you begin another, and with every book you read you change the whole plan of your interior life. Soon you will have no life at all. Your whole existence will be a patchwork of confused desires and daydreams and velleities in which you do nothing except defeat the work of grace: for all this is an elaborate subconscious device of your nature to resist God, Whose work in your soul demands the sacrifice of all that you desire and delight in, and, indeed, of all that you are.

So keep still, and let Him do some work.

This is what it means to renounce not only pleasures and possessions, but even your own self. (NS 260–261)

────────

God approaches our minds by receding from them. We can never fully know Him if we think of Him as an object of capture, to be fenced in by the enclosure of our own ideas. We know Him better after our minds have let Him go. The Lord travels in all directions at once. The Lord arrives from all directions at once.

Wherever we are, we find that He has just departed. Wherever we go, we discover that He has just arrived before us. (NM 239)

────────

It is not that someone else is preventing you from living happily; you yourself do not know what you want. Rather than admit this, you pretend that someone is keeping you from exercising your liberty. Who is this?

It is you yourself. But as long as you pretend to live in pure autonomy, as your own master, without even a god to rule you, you will inevitably live as the servant of another man or as the alienated member of an organization. Paradoxically it is the acceptance of God that makes you free and delivers you from human tyranny, for when you serve Him you are no longer permitted to alienate your spirit in human servitude. God did not *invite* the Children of Israel to leave the slavery of Egypt: He *commanded* them to do so. (NS 110)

———————

God gives us freedom to make our own lives within the situation which is the gift of His love to us, and by means of the power His love grants us. But we feel guilty about it. We are quite capable of being happy in the life He has provided for us, in which we can contend and make our own way, helped by His grace. We are ashamed to do so. For we need one thing more than happiness: we need approval. And the need for approval destroys our capacity for happiness. "How can you believe, who seek glory one from another?"[10] (CGB 84)

———————

To believe in suffering is pride: but to suffer, believing in God, is humility. For pride may tell us that we are strong enough to suffer, that suffering is good for us because we are good. Humility tells us that suffering is an evil which we must always expect to find in our lives because of the evil that is in ourselves. But faith also knows that the mercy of God is given to those who seek Him in suffering, and that by His grace we can overcome evil with good. Suffering, then, becomes good by accident, by the good that it enables us to receive more abundantly from the mercy of God. It does not make us good by itself, but it enables us to make ourselves better than we are. Thus, what we consecrate to God in suffering is not our suffering but our *selves*. (NM 78)

———————

Cartesian thought began with an attempt to reach God as object by starting from the thinking self.[11] But when God becomes object, he sooner or later "dies," because God as object is ultimately unthinkable. God as object is not only a mere abstract concept, but one which contains so many internal contradictions that it becomes entirely nonnegotiable except when it is hardened into an idol that is maintained in existence by a sheer act of will. For a long time man continued to be capable of this will-fulness: but now the effort has become exhausting and many Christians have realized it to be futile. Relaxing the effort, they have let go the "God-object" which their fathers and grandfathers still hoped to manipulate for their own ends. Their weariness has accounted for the element of resentment which made this a conscious "murder" of the deity. Liberated from the strain of willfully maintaining an object-God in existence, the Cartesian consciousness remains none the less imprisoned in itself. Hence the need to break out of itself and to meet "the other" in "encounter," "openness," "fellowship," "communion." (Z&B 23)

———————

To know anything at all of God's will we have to participate, in some manner, in the vision of the prophets: men who were always alive to the divine light concealed in the opacity of things and events, and who sometimes saw glimpses of that light where other men saw nothing but ordinary happenings. (NM 62)

———————

The Self is not its own center and does not orbit around itself; it is centered on God, the one center of all, which is "everywhere and nowhere." In whom all are encountered, from whom all proceed. Thus from the very start this consciousness is disposed to encounter "the other" with whom it is already united anyway "in God." (Z&B 24)

———————

Hope not because you think you can be good, but because God loves us irrespective of our merits and whatever is good in us comes from His love, not from our own doing. (MJ 172)

He is closer to us than we are to ourselves, although we do not see him. Whoever seeks to catch Him and hold Him loses Him. He is like the wind that blows where it pleases. You who love Him must love Him as arriving from where you do not know and as going where you do not know. Your spirit must seek to be as clean and as free as His own Spirit, in order to follow Him wherever He goes. Who are we to call ourselves either clean or free, unless He makes us so?

If He should teach us how to follow Him into the wilderness of His own freedom, we will no longer know where we are, because we are with Him Who is everywhere and nowhere at the same time.

Those who love only His apparent presence cannot follow the Lord wherever He goes. They do not love Him perfectly if they do not allow Him to be absent. They do not respect His liberty to do as He pleases. They think their prayers have made them able to command Him, and to subject His will to their own. They live on the level of magic rather than on the level of religion.

Only those men are never separated from the Lord who never question His right to separate Himself from them. They never lose Him because they always realize they never deserve to find Him, and that in spite of their unworthiness they have already found Him.

For He has first found them, and will not let them go. (NM 238)

PART FOUR

LOVE IN ACTION

Dostoyevsky wrote: "Love in action is a harsh and dread-ful thing compared to love in dreams. Love in dreams is greedy for immediate action, rapidly performed and in the sight of all."

This section explores the challenges of love in action.

TOWARD A THEOLOGY
OF LOVE

The one thing necessary is a true interior and spiritual life, true growth, on my own, in depth in a new direction. Whatever new direction God opens up for me. My job is to press forward, to grow interiorly, to pray, to break away from attachments and to defy fears, to grow in faith, which has its own solitude, to seek an entirely new perspective and new dimension in my life. To open up new horizons at any cost, to desire this and let the Holy Spirit take care of the rest. But really to desire this and work for it. (IM 144)

———————

A theology of love cannot afford to be sentimental. It cannot afford to preach edifying generalities about charity, while identifying "peace" with mere established power and legalized violence against the oppressed. A theology of love cannot be allowed merely to serve the interests of the rich and powerful, justifying their wars, their violence and their bombs, while exhorting the poor and underprivileged to practice patience, meekness, longsuffering and to solve their problems if at all, non-violently.

The theology of love must seek to deal realistically with the evil and injustice in the world, and not merely to compromise with them. Such a theology will have to take note of the ambiguous realities of politics, without embracing the specious myth of a "realism" that merely justifies force in the service of established power. Theology does not exist merely to appease the already too untroubled conscience of the powerful and the established. A theology of love may also conceivably turn out to be a theology of revolution. In any case, it is a theology of resistance, a refusal of the evil that reduces a brother to homicidal desperation. (FAV 8–9)

———————

All men seek peace first of all with themselves. That is necessary, because we do not naturally find rest even in our own being. We have to learn to commune with ourselves before we can communicate with other men and with God. A man who is not at peace with himself necessarily projects his interior fighting into the society of those he lives with, and spreads a contagion of conflict all around him. Even when he tries to do good to others his efforts are hopeless, since he does not know how to do good to himself. In moments of wildest idealism he may take it into his head to make other people happy: and in doing so he will overwhelm them with his own unhappiness. He seeks to find himself

somehow in the work of making others happy. Therefore he throws himself into the work. As a result he
gets out of the work all that he put into it: his own
confusion, his own disintegration, his own unhappiness. (NM 121)

———————

He who attempts to act and do things for others or for
the world without deepening his own self-understanding,
freedom, integrity and capacity to love, will not have
anything to give others. He will communicate to them
nothing but the contagion of his own obsessions, his
aggressiveness, his ego-centered ambitions, his delusions about ends and means, his doctrinaire prejudices and ideas. There is nothing more tragic in the
modern world than the misuse of power and action
to which men are driven by their own Faustian mis-
understandings and misapprehensions. We have more
power at our disposal today than we have ever had, and
yet we are more alienated and estranged from the inner ground of meaning and of love than we have ever
been. (CIWA 164)

———————

The basic and most fundamental problem of the spiritual life is this acceptance of our hidden and dark self,
with which we tend to identify all the evil that is in
us. We must learn by discernment to separate the evil

growth of our actions from the good ground of the soul. And we must prepare that ground so that a new life can grow up from it within us, beyond our knowledge and beyond our conscious control. The sacred attitude is then one of reverence, awe, and silence before the mystery that begins to take place within us when we become aware of our inmost self. In silence, hope, expectation, and unknowing, the man of faith abandons himself to the divine will: not as to an arbitrary and magic power whose decrees must be spelt out from cryptic ciphers, but as to the stream of reality and of life itself. The sacred attitude is then one of deep and fundamental respect for the real in whatever new form it may present itself. The secular attitude is one of gross disrespect for reality, upon which the worldly mind seeks only to force its own crude patterns. The secular man is the slave of his own prejudices, preconceptions and limitations. The man of faith is ideally free from prejudice and plastic in his uninhibited response to each new movement of the stream of life. I say "ideally" in order to exclude those whose faith is not pure but is also another form of prejudice enthroned in the exterior man—a preconceived opinion rather than a living responsiveness to the *logos* of each new situation. For there exists a kind of "hard" and rigid religious faith that is not really alive or spiritual, but resides entirely in the exterior self and is the product of conventionalism and systematic prejudice. (CQR 215–216)

Am I sure that the meaning of my life is the meaning God intends for it? Does God impose a meaning on my life from the *outside*, through event, custom, routine, law, system, impact with others in society? Or am I called to *create from within*, with him, with his grace, a meaning which reflects his truth and makes me his "word" spoken freely in my personal situation? My true identity lies hidden in God's call to my freedom and my response to him. This means I must use my freedom in order to *love*, with full responsibility and authenticity, not merely receiving a form imposed on me by external forces, or forming my own life according to an approved social pattern, but directing my love to the personal reality of my brother, and embracing God's will in its naked, often impenetrable mystery. (CTP 68)

To allow oneself to be carried away by a multitude of conflicting concerns, to surrender to too many demands, to commit oneself to too many projects, to want to help everyone in everything is to succumb to violence. More than that, it is cooperation in violence. The frenzy of the activist neutralizes his work for peace. It destroys his own inner capacity for peace. It destroys the fruitfulness of his own work, because

it kills the root of inner wisdom which makes work
fruitful. (CGB 73)

———

In moments that appear to be lucid, I tell myself that
in times like these there has to be something for which
one is *willing* to get shot, and for which, in all prob-
ability, one is actually going to get shot. What is this? A
principle? Faith? Virtue? God?

The question is not easy to answer and perhaps it
has no answer that can be put into words. Perhaps this
is no longer something communicable, or even thinkable. To be executed today (and death by execution is
not at all uncommon) one has no need to commit a
political crime, to express opposition to a tyrant, or
even to hold an objectionable opinion. indeed most
political deaths under tyrannical regimes are motive-
less, arbitrary, absurd. You are shot, or beaten to death,
or starved, or worked until you drop, not because of
anything you have done, not because of anything you
believe in, not because of anything you stand for, but
arbitrarily: your death is demanded by something or
someone undefined. Your death is necessary to give
apparent meaning to a meaningless political process
which you have never quite managed to understand.
Your death is necessary to exercise a hypothetical
influence on a hypothetical person who might con-

ceivably be opposed to something you may or may not know or understand or like or hate.

Your death is necessary not because you yourself are opposed to anything, or in favor of anything, but simply because people have to keep dying in order to make clear that opposition to those in power is neither practical nor even thinkable. Your death is necessary as a kind of exorcism of the abstract specter of opposition in the minds of leaders whose dishonesty makes them well enough aware that they ought to be opposed. Two thousand years ago the death of a Christian martyr was a supreme affirmation not only of faith, but of liberty. The Christian proved by martyrdom that he had reached a degree of independence in which it no longer mattered to him whether he lived on earth and that it was not necessary for him to save his life by paying official religious homage to the emperor. He was beyond life and death. He had attained to a condition in which all things were "one" and equal to him. (CGB 91–92)

———

I am more and more impressed by the fact that it is largely futile to get up and make statements about current problems. At the same time, I know that silent acquiescence in evil is also out of the question. I know too that there are times when protest is inescapable, even when it seems as useless as beating your head up against a brick wall. At the same time, when protest simply becomes an act of desperation, it loses its power to communicate anything to anyone who does not share the same feelings of despair.

There is of course no need to comment on the uselessness of false optimism, or to waste any attentions on the sunlit absurdities of those who consistently refuse to face reality. One cannot be a Christian today without having a deeply afflicted conscience. I say it again: we are all under judgment. And it seems to me that our gestures of repentance, though they may be individually sincere, are collectively hollow and even meaningless. Why?

This is the question that plagues me.

The reason seems to be, to some extent, a deep failure of communication. (FAV 147)

———

If I insist on giving you my truth, and never stop to receive your truth in return, then there can be no truth between us. Christ is present "where two or three are gathered in my name." But to be gathered in the name of Christ is to be gathered in the name of the Word made flesh, of God made man. It is therefore to be gathered in the faith that God has become man and can be seen in man, that he can speak in man and that he can enlighten and inspire love in and through any man

I meet. It is true that the visible Church alone has the official mission to sanctify and teach all nations, but no man knows that the stranger he meets coming out of the forest in a new country is not already an invisible member of Christ and perhaps one who has some providential or prophetic message to utter. (CP 383)

———————

We do not exist for ourselves alone, and it is only when we are fully convinced of this fact that we begin to love ourselves properly and thus also love others. What do I mean by loving ourselves properly? I mean, first of all, desiring to live, accepting life as a very great gift and a great good, not because of what it gives us, but because of what it enables us to give to others. (NM xx)

———————

If we live for others, we will gradually discover that no one expects us to be "as gods." We will see that we are human, like everyone else, that we all have weaknesses and deficiencies, and that these limitations of ours play a most important part in all our lives. It is because of them that we need others and others need us. We are not all weak in the same spots, and so we supplement and complete one another, each one making up in himself for the lack in another. (NM xxi)

———————

Our task now is to learn that if we can voyage to the ends of the earth and find ourselves in the aborigine who most differs from ourselves, we will have made a fruitful pilgrimage. That is why pilgrimage is necessary, in some shape or other. Mere sitting at home and meditating on the divine presence is not enough for our time. We have to come to the end of a long journey and see that the stranger we meet there is no other than ourselves—which is the same as saying we find Christ in him. For if the Lord is risen, as He said, He is actually or potentially alive in every man. Our pilgrimage to the Holy Sepulcher[12] is our pilgrimage to the stranger who is Christ our fellow pilgrim and brother. (M&Z 112)

———

If I can unite in myself the thought and the devotion of Eastern and Western Christendom, the Greek and the Latin Fathers, the Russians with the Spanish mystics, I can prepare in myself the reunion of divided Christians. From that secret and unspoken unity in myself can eventually come a visible and manifest unity of all Christians. If we want to bring together what is divided, we cannot do so by imposing one division upon the other or absorbing one division into the other. But if we do this, the union is not Christian. It is political, and doomed to further conflict.

We must contain all divided worlds in ourselves and transcend them in Christ. (CGB 12)

———————

Into this world, this demented inn, in which there is absolutely no room for Him at all, Christ has come uninvited. But because He cannot be at home in it, because He is out of place in it, and yet He must be in it, His place is with those others for whom there is no room. His place is with those who do not belong, who are rejected by power because they are regarded as weak, those who are discredited, who are denied the status of persons, tortured, exterminated. With those for whom there is no room, Christ is present in this world. He is mysteriously present in those for whom there seems to be nothing but the world at its worst. For them, there is no escape even in imagination. They cannot identify with the power structure of a crowded humanity which seeks to project itself outward, anywhere, in a centrifugal flight into the void, to get *out there* where there is no God, no man, no name, no identity, no weight, no self, nothing but the bright, self-directed, perfectly obedient and infinitely expensive machine. (RU 72–73)

———————

There is another kind of justice than the justice of number, which can neither forgive nor be forgiven. There is another kind of mercy than the mercy of Law which knows no absolution. There is a justice of newborn worlds which cannot be counted. There is a mercy of individual things that spring into being without reason. They are just without reason, and their mercy is without explanation. They have received rewards beyond description because they themselves refuse to be described. They are virtuous in the sight of God because their names do not identify them. Every plant that stands in the light of the sun is a saint and an outlaw. Every tree that brings forth blossoms without the command of man is powerful in the sight of God. Every star that man has not counted is a world of sanity and perfection. Every blade of grass is an angel singing in a shower of glory. (RU 106–107)

———

It is useless to try to make peace with ourselves by being pleased with everything we have done. In order to settle down in the quiet of our own being we must learn to be detached from the results of our own activity. We must withdraw ourselves, to some extent, from effects that are beyond our control and be content with the good will and the work that are the quiet expression of our inner life. We must be content to live without watching ourselves live, to work without expecting an immediate reward, to love without an instantaneous satisfaction, and to exist without any special recognition. It is only when we are detached from ourselves that we can be at peace with ourselves. We cannot find happiness in our work if we are always extending ourselves beyond ourselves and beyond the sphere of our work in order to find ourselves greater than we are. Our Christian destiny is, in fact, a great one: but we cannot achieve greatness unless we lose all interest in being great. For our own idea of greatness is illusory. (NM 121)

––––––

There is a certain innocence in not having a solution. There is a certain innocence in a kind of despair: but only if in despair we find salvation. I mean, despair of this world and what is in it. Despair of men and of their plans, in order to hope for the impossible answer that lies beyond our earthly contradictions, and yet can burst into our world and solve them only if there are some who hope in spite of despair. The true solutions are not those which we force upon in accordance with our theories, but those which life itself provides for those who dispose themselves to receive the truth. Consequently our task is to dissociate ourselves from all who have theories which promise clear and infallible solutions, and to mistrust all such theories not in a spirit of negativism and defeat, but rather trusting life itself, and nature, and if you will permit me, God above all. For since man has decided to occupy the place of God he has shown himself to be far the blindest, and cruelest, and pettiest and most ridiculous of all the false gods. We can call ourselves innocent only if we refuse to forget this, and if we also do everything we can to make others realize it. (RU 60–61)

NONVIOLENCE

Nonviolence is perhaps the most exacting of all forms of struggle, not only because it demands first of all that one be ready to suffer evil and even face the threat of death without violent retaliation, but because it excludes mere transient self-interest from its considerations. In a very real sense, he who practices nonviolent resistance must commit himself not to the defense of his own interests or even those of a particular group: he must commit himself to the defense of objective truth and right and above all of *man*. His aim is then not simply to "prevail" or to prove that he is right and the adversary wrong, or to make the adversary give in and yield what is demanded of him. Nor should the nonviolent resister be content to prove to *himself* that *he* is virtuous and right, and that *his* hands and heart are pure even though the adversary's may be evil and defiled. Still less should he seek for himself the psychological gratification of upsetting the adversary's conscience and perhaps driving him to an act of bad faith and refusal of the truth. We know that our unconscious motives may, at times, make our nonviolence a form of moral aggression and even a subtle provocation designed (without our awareness) to bring out the evil we hope to find in the adversary, and thus to justify our selves in our own eyes and in the eyes of "decent people." (PP 249)

———

Has nonviolence been found wanting? Yes and no. It has been found wanting wherever it has been the nonviolence of the weak. It has not been found wanting when it has been the nonviolence of the strong. What is the difference? It is a difference of language. The language of spurious nonviolence is merely another, more equivocal form of the language of power. It is used and conceived pragmatically, in reference to the seizure of power. But that is not what nonviolence is about. Nonviolence is not for power but for truth. It is not pragmatic but prophetic. It is not aimed at immediate political results, but at the manifestation of fundamental and crucially important truth. Nonviolence is not primarily the language of efficacy, but the language of *kairos*.[13] It does not say, "We shall overcome" so much as "This is the day of the Lord, and whatever may happen to us, *He* shall overcome." (LE 28)

———

There can be no question that unless war is abolished the world will remain constantly in a state of madness and desperation in which, because of the immense destructive power of modern weapons, the danger of catastrophe will be imminent and probably at every moment everywhere. Unless we set ourselves immediately to this task, both as individuals and in our political and religious groups, we tend by our passivity and fatalism to cooperate with the destructive forces that are leading inexorably to war. It is a problem of terrifying complexity and magnitude, for which the Church herself is not fully able to see clear and decisive solutions. Yet she must lead the way on the road towards nonviolent settlement of difficulties and towards the gradual abolition of war as the way of settling international or civil disputes. Christians must become active in every possible way, mobilizing all their resources for the fight against war. First of all there is much to be studied, much to be learned. Peace is to be preached, nonviolence is to be explained as a practical method, and not left to be mocked as an outlet for crackpots who want to make a show of themselves. Prayers and sacrifice must be used as the most effective spiritual weapons in the war against war, and like all weapons they must be used with deliberate aim: not just with a vague aspiration for peace and security, but against violence and against war. This implies that we are also willing to sacrifice and restrain our own instinct for violence and aggressiveness in our relations with other people. We may never succeed in this campaign, but whether we succeed or not the duty is evident. It is the great Christian task of our time. Everything else is secondary, for the survival of the human race itself depends upon it. We must at least face this responsibility and do something about it. And the first job of all is to understand the psychological forces at work in ourselves and in society. (RW 1)

———————

Nonviolence must be aimed above all at the transformation of the present state of the world, and it must therefore be free from all occult, unconscious connivance with an unjust use of power. This poses enormous problems—for if nonviolence is too political it becomes drawn into the power struggle and identified with one side or another in that struggle, while if it is totally apolitical it runs the risk of being ineffective or at best merely symbolic. (PP 253)

———————

Nonviolence seeks to "win" not by destroying or even by humiliating the adversary, but by *convincing him* that there is a higher and more certain common good than can be attained by bombs and blood. Non-violence, ideally speaking, does not try to overcome the adversary by winning over him, but to turn him from an adversary into a collaborator by winning him over. Unfortunately, non-violent resistance as practiced by those who do not understand it and have not been trained in it, is often only a weak and veiled form of psychological aggression. (FAV 12–13)

———————

Nonviolence must avoid the ambiguity of an unclear and *confusing protest* that hardens the war makers in their self-righteous blindness. This means in fact that *in this case above all nonviolence must avoid* a *facile and fanatical self-righteousness,* and refrain from being satisfied with dramatic self-justifying gestures.

Perhaps the most insidious temptation to be avoided is one which is characteristic of the power structure itself: this fetishism of immediate visible results. Modern society understands "possibilities" and "results" in terms of a superficial and quantitative idea of efficacy. One of the missions of Christian nonviolence is to restore a different standard of practical judgment in social conflicts. This means that the Christian humility of nonviolent action must establish itself in the minds and memories of modern man not only as *conceivable* and *possible*, but as a *desirable alternative* to what he now considers the only realistic possibility: namely, political technique backed by force. Here the human dignity of nonviolence must manifest itself clearly in terms of a freedom and a nobility which are able to resist political manipulation and brute force and show them up as arbitrary, barbarous, and irrational. This will not be easy. The temptation to get publicity and quick results by spectacular tricks or by forms of protest that are merely odd and provocative but whose human meaning is not clear may defeat this purpose. (PP 253–254)

———

Strong hate, the hate that takes joy in hating, is strong because it does not believe itself to be unworthy and alone. It feels the support of a justifying God, of an idol of war, an avenging and destroying spirit. From such blood-drinking gods the human race was once liberated, with great toil and terrible sorrow, by the death of a God Who delivered Himself to the Cross and suffered the pathological cruelty of His own creatures out of pity for them. In conquering death He opened their eyes to the reality of a love which asks no questions about worthiness, a love which overcomes hatred and destroys death. But men have now come to reject this divine revelation of pardons and they are consequently returning to the old war gods, the god that insatiably drink blood and eat the flesh of men. It is easier to serve the hate-gods because they thrive on the worship of collective fanaticism. To serve the hate-gods, one has only to be blinded by collective passion. To serve the God of Love one must be free, one must face the terrible responsibility of the decision to love *in spite of all unworthiness* whether in oneself or in one's neighbor. (NS 73–74)

Instead of trying to use the adversary as leverage for one's own effort to realize an ideal, nonviolence seeks only to enter into a dialogue with him in order to attain, together with him, the common good of *man*. Nonviolence must be realistic and concrete. Like ordinary political action, it is no more than the "art of the possible." But precisely the advantage of nonviolence is that it has a *more Christian and more humane notion of what is possible.* Where the powerful believe that only power is efficacious, the nonviolent resister is persuaded of the superior efficacy of love, openness, peaceful negotiation, and above all of truth. For power can guarantee the interests of *some men* but it can never foster the good of *man*. Power always protects the good of some at the expense of all the others. Only love can attain and preserve the good of all. Any claim to build the security of *all* on force is a manifest imposture. (PP 254)

A test of our sincerity in the practice of nonviolence is this: Are we willing to *learn something from the adversary?* If a *new truth* is made known to us by him or through him, will we accept it? Are we willing to admit that he is not totally inhumane, wrong, unreasonable, cruel, etc.? This is important. If he sees that we are completely incapable of listening to him with an open mind, our nonviolence will have nothing to say to him except that we distrust him and seek to outwit him. Our readiness to see some good in him and to agree with some of his ideas (though tactically this might look like a weakness on our part), actually gives us power: the power of sincerity and of truth. On the other hand, if we are obviously unwilling to accept any truth that we have not first discovered and declared ourselves, we show by that very fact that we are interested not in the truth so much as in "being right." Since the adversary is presumably interested in being right also, and in proving himself right by what he considers the superior argument of force, we end up where we started. Nonviolence has great power, provided that it really witnesses to truth and not just to self-righteousness.

The dread of being open to the ideas of others generally comes from our hidden insecurity about our own convictions. We fear that we may be "converted"—or perverted by a pernicious doctrine. On the other hand, if we are mature and objective in our open-mindedness, we may find that viewing things from a basically different perspective—that of our adversary—we discover our own truth in a new light and are able to understand our own ideal more realistically. (PP 255)

Wherever there is a high moral ideal there is an attendant risk of pharisaism, and nonviolence is no exception. The basis of pharisaism is division: on one hand this morally or socially privileged self and the elite to which it belongs. On the other hand, the "others," the wicked, the unenlightened, whoever they may be, Communists, capitalists, colonialists, traitors, international Jewry, racists, etc.

Christian nonviolence is not built on a presupposed division, but on the basic unity of man. It is not out for the conversion of the wicked to the ideas of the good, but for the healing and reconciliation of man with himself, man the person, and man the human family. (PP 249)

The nonviolent resister is not fighting simply for "his" truth or for "his" pure conscience, or for the right that is on "his side." On the contrary, both his strength and his weakness come from the fact that he is fighting for the truth, common to him and to the adversary, the right which is objective and universal. He is fighting for everybody. (FAV 15–16)

Do not be too quick to assume your enemy is a savage just because he is *your* enemy. Perhaps he is your enemy because he thinks you are a savage. Or perhaps he is afraid of you because he feels that you are afraid of him. And perhaps if he believed you were capable of loving him he would no longer be your enemy.

Do not be too quick to assume that your enemy is an enemy of God just because he is *your* enemy. Perhaps he is your enemy precisely because he can find nothing in you that gives glory to God. Perhaps he fears you because he can find nothing in you of God's love and God's kindness and God's patience and mercy and understanding of the weaknesses of men.

Do not be too quick to condemn the man who no longer believes in God, for it is perhaps your own coldness and avarice, your mediocrity and materialism, your sensuality and selfishness that have killed his faith. (NS 177)

————————

The hope of the Christian must be, like the hope of a child, pure and full of trust. The child is totally available in the present because he has relatively little to remember, his experience of evil is as yet brief, and his anticipation of the future does not extend far. The Christian, in his humility and faith, must be as totally available to his brother, to his world, in the present, as the child is. But he cannot see the world with childlike innocence and simplicity unless his memory is cleared of past evils by forgiveness, and his anticipation of the future is hopefully free of craft and calculation. For this reason, the humility of Christian nonviolence is at once patient and uncalculating. The chief difference between nonviolence and violence is that the latter depends entirely on its own calculations. The former depends entirely on God and on His word. (PP 257–258)

SAINTHOOD

When Lax and I were walking down Sixth Avenue, one night in the spring, the street was all torn up and trenched and banked high with dirt and marked out with red lanterns where they were digging the subway, and we picked our way along the fronts of the dark little stores, going downtown to Greenwich Village.[14] I forget what we were arguing about, but in the end Lax suddenly turned around and asked me the question:

"What do you want to be, anyway?"

I could not say, "I want to be Thomas Merton the well-known writer of all those book reviews in the back pages of the *Times Book Review*," or "Thomas Merton the assistant instructor of Freshman English at the New Life Social Institute for Progress and Culture," so I put the thing on the spiritual plane, where I knew it belonged and said:

"I don't know; I guess what I want is to be a good Catholic."

"What do you mean, you want to be a good Catholic?"

The explanation I gave was lame enough, and expressed my confusion, and betrayed how little I had really thought about it at all.

Lax did not accept it.

"What you should say"—he told me— "what you should say is that you want to be a saint."

A saint! The thought struck me as a little weird. I said: "How do you expect me to become a saint?"

"By wanting to," said Lax, simply.

"I can't be a saint," I said, "I can't be a saint." And my mind darkened with a confusion of realities and unrealities: the knowledge of my own sins, and the false humility which makes men say that they cannot do the things that they *must* do, cannot reach the level that they *must* reach: the cowardice that says: "I am satisfied to save my soul, to keep out of mortal sin," but which means, by those words: "I do not want to give up my sins and my attachments."

But Lax said: "No. All that is necessary to be a saint is to want to be one. Don't you believe that God will make you what He created you to be, if you will consent to let Him do it? All you have to do is desire it." (SSM 237–238)

———

We tend to think of "the martyrs" as men of a different stamp from ourselves, men of another age, bred in another atmosphere, men somehow stronger and greater than we. But it turns out that we too are expected to face the same sufferings and confess Christ and die for Him. We who are not heroes are the ones God is choosing to share the lot of His great warriors. And one look into our own souls tells us that there is nothing there that invites the combats of the mighty saints. There is nothing magnificent about us. We are miserable things and if we are called upon to die we shall die miserably. There is nothing of grandeur about us. We are null. And perhaps we are already marked for sacrifice—a sacrifice that will be, in the eyes of the world, perhaps only drab and sorry and mean. And yet it will end by being our greatest glory after all. Perhaps there is no greater glory than to be reduced to insignificance by an unjust and stupid temporal power, in order that God may triumph over evil through our insignificance. (SOJ 79)

———

Some men have been picked out to bear witness to Christ's love in lives overwhelmed by suffering. These have proclaimed that suffering was their vocation. But that should not lead us to believe that in order to be a saint one must go out for suffering in the same way that a college athlete goes out for football. No two men have to suffer exactly the same trials in exactly the same way. No one man is ever called to suffer merely for the sake of suffering. (NM 80)

The saint is not one who accepts suffering because he likes it, and confesses this preference before God and men in order to win a great reward. He is one who may well hate suffering as much as anybody else, but who so loves Christ, Whom he does not see, that he will allow His love to be proved by any suffering. And he does this not because he thinks it is an achievement, but because the charity of Christ in his heart demands that it be done. (NM 79–80)

———

The saint, therefore, is sanctified not only by fasting when he should fast but also by eating when he should eat. He is not only sanctified by his prayers in the darkness of the night, but by the sleep that he takes in obedience to God, Who made us what we are. Not only His solitude contributes to his union with God, but also his supernatural love for his friends and his relatives and those with whom he lives and works. (NM 99)

———

One of the first signs of a saint may well be the fact that other people do not know what to make of him. In fact, they are not sure whether he is crazy or only proud; but it must at least be pride to be haunted by some individual ideal which nobody but God really comprehends. And he has inescapable difficulties in applying all the abstract norms of "perfection" to his own life. He cannot seem to make his life fit in with the books. Sometimes his case is so bad that no monastery will keep him. He has to be dismissed, sent back to the world like Benedict Joseph Labre, who wanted to be a Trappist and a Carthusian and succeeded in neither. He finally ended up as a tramp. He died in some street in Rome. And yet the only canonized saint, venerated by the whole Church, who has lived either as a Cistercian or a Carthusian since the Middle Ages is St. Benedict Joseph Labre. (NS 103)

———

The saints are what they are, not because their sanctity makes them admirable to others, but because the gift of sainthood makes it possible for them to admire everybody else. (NS 57)

———

For me to be a saint means to be myself. Therefore the problem of sanctity and salvation is in fact the problem of finding out who I am and of discovering my true self. Trees and animals have no problem. God makes them what they are without consulting them, and they are perfectly satisfied. With us it is different.

God leaves us free to be whatever we like. We can be ourselves or not, as we please. We are at liberty to be real, or to be unreal. We may be true or false, the choice is ours. We may wear now one mask and now another, and never, if we desire, appear with our own true face. But we cannot make these choices with impunity. Causes have effects, and if we lie to ourselves and to others, then we cannot expect to find truth and reality whenever we happen to want them. If we have chosen the way of falsity we must not be surprised that truth eludes us when we finally come to need it! (NS 31–32)

––––––––

Be content that you are not a saint, even though you realize that the only thing worth living for is sanctity. Then you will be satisfied to let God lead you to sanctity by paths that you cannot understand. You will travel in darkness in which you will no longer be concerned with yourself and no longer compare yourself to other men. Those who have gone by that way have finally found out that sanctity is in everything and that God is all around them. Having given up all desire to compete with other men, they suddenly wake up and find that the joy of God is everywhere, and they are able to exult in the virtues and goodness of others more than ever they could have done in their own. They are so dazzled by the reflection of God in the souls of the men they live with that they no longer have any power to condemn anything they see in another. Even in the greatest sinners they can see virtues and goodness that no one else can find. As for themselves, if they still consider themselves, they no longer dare to compare themselves with others. The idea has now become unthinkable. But it is no longer a source of suffering and lamentation: they have finally reached the point where they take their own insignificance for granted. They are no longer interested in their external selves. (NS 59–60)

NOTES

1. Merton admired Father Paul Evdokimov's essay on the Desert Fathers, particularly the line "one goes into the desert to vomit up the interior phantom, the doubter, the double." (CGB 309)

2. Tantalus was a legendary Greek King of Lydia who was punished for offenses against the gods by being made to stand in Hades within reach of food and drink that moved away whenever he tried to touch them.

3. Alan Harrington's book published in 1959 was a minor masterpiece of social criticism, exposing the psychological costs of what was then called "the rat race."

4. Dietrich Bonhoeffer (1906–1945) Protestant theologian who identified himself with the German Confessing Church which opposed the pro-Nazi part of the Lutheran Church. During the war he became involved with anti-Hitler conspirators. He was arrested by the Nazis and hung in Buchenwald concentration camp. His posthumous letters—along with his book The Cost of Discipleships—explored the role of Christian ethics in a world "come of age."

5. Writing at the height of the Cold War, the "adversary" Merton is referring to is the USSR.

6. In classical Greek thought "nature" had two aspects: the passive reality of our daily experience (*natura naturata* or rested nature) and the active power that directs and governs life as well as the growth of a work

7. Greek for "Holy Wisdom."

8. Matthew 16:25

9. Literally, "virginal time" first flowering.

10. John 5:44

11. Named after the French philosopher Rene Descartes (1596–1650), Cartesian thought refers to the line of inquiry that extends the mathematical method into all realms of knowledge in the search for certainty. Beginning with universal doubt, Descartes believed that the only thing that could not be doubted was his own thinking; hence the famous Cartesian maxim: "I think; therefore, I am."

12. Site of the crucifixion, death, burial and resurrection of Jesus.

13. Greek word referring to "the fullness of time." The propitious moment for the performance of an action or the coming into being of a new state. The time of urgent and providential decision.

14. "Lax" is Robert Lax who later converted to Catholicism and became known for his experimental poetry.

SOURCES

(AJ) *The Asian Journal of Thomas Merton,* ed. Naomi Burton, Brother Patrick Hart, and James Laughlin (New York: New Directions, 1973)

(ATT) *The Ascent to Truth* (New York: Harcourt, Brace, 1951)

(BIW) *Bread in the Wilderness* (New York: New Directions, 1953)

(CFT) *The Courage for Truth: Letters to Writers,* ed. Christine M. Bochen (New York: Farrar, Straus & Giroux, 1993)

(CGB) *Conjectures of a Guilty Bystander* (New York: Doubleday, 1966)

(CIWA) *Contemplation in a World of Action* (New York: Doubleday, 1971)

(CTP) *Contemplative Prayer* (New York, Doubleday, 1969)

(CNP) *Centering Prayer* by Basil Pennington (Garden City, New York, Doubleday, 1980)

(CP) *The Collected Poems of Thomas Merton* (New York: New Directions, 1977)

(CQR) *Cistercian Quarterly Review* #18 (1983)

(DQ) *Disputed Questions* (New York: Farrar, Straus, and Cudahy, 1960)

(FAV) *Faith and Violence* (Notre Dame; University of Notre Dame Press, 1968)

(HR) *"Honorable Reader": Reflections on My Work,* ed. Robert E. Daggy (New York: Crossroad, 1989)

(IM) *The Intimate Merton: His Life from His Journals* ed. By Patrick Hart and Jonathan Montaldo (San Francisco, Harper SF, 1999)

(LE) *The Literary Essays of Thomas Merton* ed. Patrick Hart (New York: New Directions, 1981)

(LL) *Love and Living,* ed. Naomi Burton Stone and Brother Patrick Hart (New York: Farrar, Straus & Giroux, 1979)

(MJ) *The Monastic Journey* edited by Brother Patrick Hart (Kansas City: Sheed, Andrews 1978)

(M&Z) *Mystics and Zen Masters* (New York: Farrar, Straus & Giroux, 1967)

(NM) *No Man Is an Island* (New York: Harcourt Brace, 1955)

(NS) *New Seeds of Contemplation* (New York: New Directions, 1962)

(OTB) *Opening the Bible* (Collegeville, Minn: Liturgical Press 1970)

(PP) *Passion for Peace: The Social Essays,* ed. William H. Shannon (New York: Crossroad, 1995)

(RU) *Raids on the Unspeakable* (New York, New Directions, 1964)

(RW) "The Root of War" in *The Catholic Worker* #28 Oct. 1961

(SD&M) *Spiritual Direction and Meditation* (Wheathampstead-Hertfordshire: Athony Clarke, 1987)

(SJ) *The Secular Journal of Thomas Merton* (New York: Harcourt, Brace, Jovanovich, 1959)

(SOJ) *Sign of Jonas* (New York: Harcourt, Brace, Jovanovich, 1953)

(SSM) *The Seven Storey Mountain* (New York: Harcourt, Brace, Jovanovich, 1948)

(TIS) *Thoughts in Solitude* (New York: Farrar, Straus, 1958)

(WOD) *Wisdom of the Desert* (New York: New Directions, 1961)

(Z&B) *Zen and the Birds of Appetite* (New York, New Directions, 1968)

CREDITS

The Pocket Thomas Merton is an abridged edition of *Seeds* first published by Shambhala Publications in 2002. Grateful acknowledgment is made to the following publishers for permission to reprint from copyrighted material:

Cistercian Publications for selections from *The Climate of Monastic Prayer* (Kalamazoo, Mich.: Cistercian Publications, 1971), also published as *Contemplative Prayer.*

Cistercian Studies Quarterly for selections from "The Inner Experience" by Thomas Merton. *Cistercian Studies Quarterly,* vols. 17 and 19, copyright by the Trustees of the Merton Legacy Trust.

Crossroad Publishing Company for *Passion for Peace: The Social Essays,* by Thomas Merton, edited by William H. Shannon (New York: Crossroad Press, 1995), copyright by the Trustees of the Merton Legacy Trust.

Doubleday, a division of Random House, for selections from *Centering Prayer* by M. Basil Pennington, copyright 1980 by the Cistercian Abbey of Spencer, Inc.; *Conjectures of a Guilty Bystander,* by Thomas Merton (Garden City, N.Y.: Doubleday, 1966), copyright by the Abbey of Our Lady of Gethsemani.

New Directions, 1963), copyright by the Abbey of Our Lady of Gethsemani; *New Seeds of Contemplation* by Thomas Merton (New York: New Directions, 1961), copyright by the Abbey of Our Lady of Gethsemani; *The Literary Essays of Thomas Merton,* by Thomas Merton, edited by Patrick Hart (New York: New Directions, 1981), copyright 1960, 1966, 1967, 1968, 1973, 1975, 1978, 1981 by the Trustees of Merton Legacy Trust; copyright 1959, 1961, 1963, 1964, 1965, 1981 by the Abbey of Our Lady of Gethsemani; copyright 1953 by Our Lady of Gethsemani Monastery.

University of Notre Dame Press for selections from *Contemplation in a World of Action,* by Thomas Merton, copyright 1998 by the University of Notre Dame Press; *Faith and Violence* by Thomas Merton (Notre Dame, Md.: University of Notre Dame Press, 1984), copyright 1984 by the University of Notre Dame Press.

The Liturgical Press for selections from *Opening the Bible,* by Thomas Merton (Collegeville, Minn.: Liturgical Press, 1970), copyright 1986 by The Order of St. Benedict, Inc.

Sheed and Ward for selections from *The Monastic Journey,* edited by Brother Patrick Hart (Kansas City, Mo.: Sheed, Andrews 1–78).

HarperSanFrancisco for a selection from *The Intimate Merton: His Life from His Journals,* edited by Patrick Hart and Jonathan Montaldo (San Francisco: HarperSanFrancisco, 1999), copyright by the Merton Legacy Trust.

The Merton Legacy Trust for a selection from *Honorable Reader: Reflections on My Work* by Thomas Merton, edited by Robert Daggy (New York: Crossroad, 1991).

SHAMBHALA POCKET LIBRARY

_____

THE POCKET CHÖGYAM TRUNGPA
Compiled and edited by Carolyn Rose Gimian

THE POCKET DALAI LAMA
Edited by Mary Craig

THE POCKET PEMA CHÖDRÖN
Edited by Eden Steinberg

THE POCKET RUMI
Edited by Kabir Helminski

THE POCKET THICH NHAT HANH
Compiled and edited by Melvin McLeod

THE POCKET THOMAS MERTON
Edited by Robert Inchausti